LET'S EXPLORE WORSHIP

LET'S EXPLORE WORSHIP

*An Activity Program Created by the Pupils
for Church School Worship*

Compiled by

EDNA EASTWOOD

MOREHOUSE-GORHAM CO.
New York
1952

Copyright, 1952, by
Morehouse-Gorham Co.

PRINTED IN THE UNITED STATES OF AMERICA
BY THE HADDON CRAFTSMEN, INC., SCRANTON, PA.

Dedicated

to

The boys and girls and leaders

Who made this book possible

and to

All who dare to be creative evangelists

for the

World of today and tomorrow

FOREWORD

"What do you think of it?"

It was a question the Rector asked me after the Church School worship service. I was Director of Religious Education. We were both new in the parish, but we were former co-workers who could speak frankly to each other. I knew he wanted an honest answer for the good of the boys and girls we had undertaken to serve.

"I think that for most of them the service of worship was an endurance test of duty, judging by the unholy rush to get out of the church at the close of the service," I answered.

The service had been well and reverently led, carefully planned for the Church season, but it had definitely not seemed to connect up with the boys' and girls' capacity for worship. I had noticed the same thing often in my traveling as a diocesan and national educational worker. Valuable life was being lost.

"What can we do about it?" queried the Rector, after agreeing with my observation.

"Ask the boys and girls about it?" I suggested.

And that is what we did, not realizing that it would eventually affect all the life of the parish with a new vitality beyond our hopes.

This is the story of what happened in a typical suburban parish of about seven hundred active members in a Church School with an average attendance of about a hundred and fifty. It is not a story of increased attendance and greater offerings, although these resulted as the interest grew. It is a story of what happened when boys and girls went exploring into the meanings and reasons and joy of worship until this joy became their own. It can be tried with spiritual profit wherever there are a few dedicated leaders who have sympathy and trust for boys and girls and a realization that the young people's part in the creation of the kingdom of heaven will continue, beyond ours, into the great Church of the future which the world needs. Because it is a creative program it is not one which can be superimposed by adults, although adult guidance and wisdom are necessary and are desired by the boys and girls. Because the program is creative it will result differently in each church, according to that church's basic beliefs and guidance, for each boy and girl thinks differently depending on how God and we ourselves have led them. The experiments, as outlined, are meant only as guides for and encouragement with your own group's adventures in worship. If you are already trying similar experiments you may find here and there a new idea your boys and girls may want to test out for themselves in their own way in order to make it real and vital.

Because this story is about some boys and girls in an Episcopal church, it must be told as it happened in that Church, to be a truthful report. However, the basic methods may be followed in any form of worship with any group of boys and girls, once the young people realize that you are allowing them their creative privilege, and challenging them to accept and explore it under the supervision of their own ministers.

Worship, and the joy of it, are universal, but many people have yet to discover the richness of worship and none have fully discovered it, nor will they, until the experience of the next life reveals it. These boys and girls found a way towards its reality and they had fun doing it. We all shared this joy with them.

—EDNA EASTWOOD

CONTENTS

LET'S EXPLORE WORSHIP

I. THE BOYS AND GIRLS EXPERIMENT WITH THEIR OWN PROBLEM

1. THE CHURCH SCHOOL STUDENT COUNCIL

A teachers' and officers' meeting was called. The members present, having suffered through many so-called services of Church School worship, agreed with the verdict the Rector and I had talked over. The worship, although satisfying to adults, was not interesting the pupils. Something should be changed. They agreed that the pupils might be the best source of information to help with any changes.

Each teacher was requested to co-operate by allowing class time to elect, not appoint, a class member for each grade above the third. This member was to represent the class at a Church School Student council meeting to be held the following week. Each class was also to be asked to think about what they liked and didn't like about their Church School. These observations were to be given (unsigned) to their council representative for reporting and discussion.

At the first meeting of the Student Council the way a council worked by sharing ideas and adopting those chosen and approved by the majority of votes, was explained. They were told how they might have the assistance of the teachers, parents and staff for any of their ideas which were finally approved by the Rector. They were also told why the Rector's approval was a courtesy which we owed to him and how, having chosen him as our Church leader, he would probably receive any criticism there might be of our actions.

They recognized the justice of this. They were willing to abide by his final decisions if they could try out the council plan of self-government and suggest ways of making the Church School more interesting. They seemed willing to trust him because he was showing his trust in them. This seemed to establish a new relationship of possible partnership. It was the first value and one which the Rector carefully nourished, although I knew that at times he must have had qualms about the wisdom of the pupils' decisions and the reactions of the adults. Being a father, he knew the possibilities both ways.

The students, themselves, suggested that, because of the difference in ages, they needed to meet as one council but with two departments for discussion. This created a senior group of representatives from the seventh grade and older, and a junior group from the three lower grades. They elected their council officers, brought this to a vote and then divided to elect a chairman for each department.

From then on, the pupils ran their own meetings. They discussed my suggestion that God would like to help them if they wanted to ask Him. This resulted in each meeting being opened with prayers which they made up themselves. They began to realize the joy of creativeness in worship and to apply it in this way to the reality of their problems.

At each meeting the minutes of the last meeting were read and the activities between the monthly meetings evaluated in a simple way. This filtered out the things the majority liked, the things they liked but needed to change or improve, and also the things that proved unpopular with the school group. Class representatives were asked to report reactions and did so very frankly and honestly, in a way which older groups find difficult because of social inhibitions.

Before they separated into departments for discussion, the director and the one teacher, whom they allowed to attend the council meetings, were asked to present problems from the teachers, parents, or officers. These were noted down for department discussion. It was soon discovered that if two typed copies were presented and read by the chairmen of each department, the discussions and their decisions were more helpful and less confusing. The adults were only used as counsellors, when requested, after the typed reports were presented. We soon discovered that the boys and girls were counselling us instead, and with much wisdom and enlightenment. They felt very important and they were—more so than they realized.

At the close of each meeting the departments came together and each presented reports of their discussions. From these, council decisions were formulated for the whole school. Sometimes class representatives were requested to bring things up for a class vote and to report at the next monthly meeting. If things had to be decided sooner than that, a council committee was appointed to receive the results and to act on them. From this the pupils learned patience with the often slower process of democratic procedure, also they liked the importance of getting the class vote. As the council representatives were chosen for only a period of three months at a time, it became both a training process and a sought-for honor. This gradually had its effect on class attitudes. It also had its effect on individual aggressive attitudes—an effect which only groups of their own age and interests could have secured. Once they realized the value of simple parliamentary procedure they required co-operation and respect for it. They dealt with each question very solemnly and decisively and the counsellor's only value was to verify some point in answer to an argument, when he was requested to do so.

Realizing that valuable material for the parents was appearing in council discussions, the pupils were asked whether or not they would like to report regularly to a group of parents and teachers. They were eager to do so and decided to send a different representative each month with copies of their minutes. This meant a more careful keeping of minutes.

A meeting of parents and teachers was called. A previous meeting of parents for a national speaker had netted twelve. The group of fathers and mothers who turned out to discuss the council's requests and findings grew to over sixty as an average monthly attendance and, during Lent or for special needs (pageants, etc.) frequent meetings of the mothers were held, and their ability was much appreciated.

At each evening parents' meeting, held monthly, the chosen council representative presented the council's requests and findings as the first item on the agenda. Then the representative was excused in order to avoid a late homecoming for him or her and also to leave the adult group free for discussion and action on the representative's report. This report was the main item of business for the parents and for the teachers.

The results were amazing in providing interesting discussion for teachers, parents, and the vestry—the governing body of the Church group. The attendance grew and committees volunteered for extra work. Like many Church Schools we lacked physical equipment and the right building arrangements for good teaching. The appeal was strong when boys and girls told how noise from another class made it hard to hear, how tables wobbled, chairs were too high for comfort, opportunities for handwork were needed, places to hang their handwork were lacking. When contrasts were made with public school facilities it alerted the adults to action. Funds were lacking for anything drastic in the way of new buildings, but time and energy might do wonders with what was available. These things made live discussion. Their own children were concerned with it.

In return, problems from the adults were presented to the council for pupil consideration and action. Fellowship between the two groups grew and, with it, a new desire on the part of each to serve the other, not just to use them. A sense of ownership of Church property ended its thoughtless use and destruction, and created a desire to improve it.

A request by the boys for men teachers sent some of the fathers and vestrymen into training. One teacher's class discussion on how our Lord fulfilled Boy Scout laws showed that previously some pupils had conceived of Him as effeminate because He had been presented to them chiefly by women teachers. The men realized the spiritual as well as the physical need for men to teach the boys. They also realized their own lack of training to meet that need.

A request for more class privacy in the large room which accommodated, necessarily, several classes, resulted in a discussion of "good" enthusiastic noise and "bad" undisciplined noise—noise itself was not necessarily "bad" in any class but too much unenthusiastic quiet might be. A suppressed class was not necessarily one that was growing spiritually. The opposite might be true. A second result was a vote of funds from the vestry to buy materials, and also a father's gift of his unemployed time and labor to make some moveable wall-board screens. These screens proved valuable in many other ways for pageants, plays, bazaars, etc. They were the usual eight-foot lengths, mounted in wooden frames to keep them from warping. Two cross-pieces with four casters made them easily movable and they could be stacked in a corner when the space was needed for a recreation or assembly hall. Blackboard cloth and thumb-tacks made the places desired for mounting handwork or pictures. Slides could be shown on them by any class with a projector. They shut out the sight and most of the noise of other classes and, in many ways, were preferable to walls.

Pageants brought both mothers and fathers into action for costumes and staging, but the plans were made by the pupils, and the parents carried out only the suggestions accepted by the pupils. Mutual appreciation resulted.

A teacher's request for an occasional Sunday off to visit her out-of-town relatives resulted in the council and the parents deciding to release all the teachers on one Sunday a month. On this Sunday it was decided to have a full Church service, and a talk either by one of the pupils, by a visiting speaker, or by the Rector. The parents consented to take turns sitting with the classes as teacher substitutes, but all the parents were invited to these special services. This resulted in more faithful attendance and work by the teachers, many of whom preferred to attend the special services. They felt more free, and they arranged absences to fit the schedule with more benefit than previously for the class sessions. (An outline of the topics chosen for these services is explained later with the class work necessary in creating them.)

A request from the classes and teachers for more mission-ary and other information for some of these services, at which the pupils gave addresses, was brought to the parents.

This resulted in the mothers meeting on two afternoons a month as a clipping bureau to compile up-to-date news in scrapbooks for the older pupils, also to prepare handwork for the busy primary and kindergarten teachers, under their direction. All of this was very enlightening for the mothers. It made missions the topic at many local bridge parties and family gatherings, and alerted everyone to watch for news.

The parents appreciated the wall-board screens when they divided up into committees. One section collected news on a certain mission field, another on a different one, a third watched for social action that was Christian or unchristian, a fourth studied costumes, a fifth either made costumes or properties. The large room became a sectional hum that later converged and shared interests during a tea prepared by rotating committees.

The death of a lone "shut-in" brought up the need for more Christian education for the older group. During Lent some of the mothers took notes on the Rector's week-day talks on the study book. Funds were not available for postage, so some of the mothers typed carbon copies, and each woman took three or more copies either to take or mail, at her own expense, to "shut-ins." Some of the older pupils, hearing of the need, later did most of the typing, and pupils of all ages learned to run the small mimeograph for various parish needs for all ages. They had so much fun drawing cartoons to make the letters interesting, that they decided to edit a school paper. (More about this will be explained later.)

The reason for all this parent activity and interest was that their own boys and girls were doing the asking, and it all became personal and vital. As the need for a mailing list frequently became necessary, individuals offered to keep the list up-to-date and run the addressograph or type the envelopes. An office committee and a car corps were two other activities. The car was used for school observation trips and by the director in calling at the homes.

Teachers' absences were rare even on their "Sundays off." It all became more interesting for them too. However, the main effect was on worship. And this new interest in worship affected all the parish life for all ages and in many ways. The "unholy rush" now was turned towards, instead of away from Church. As soon as the public school closed the parish house was teaming with noisy, happy, constructively occupied boys and girls. They were eager to come and loath to leave even when hungry for suppers at home.

Many things were happening at the same time, although each must be told about separately. An important result of the council's discussion was the free and constructive criticism of lessons, courses, equipment, ritual, attitudes, furnishings, etc.

We found that the young people wanted many things. Among them were the following:

> More variety in their programs.
> More knowledge of how and why in their ritual.
> More comfortable equipment for worship, such as higher or double-kneeling hassocks for the shorter boys and girls, both for their feet when seated and also to see what the leaders were doing at services such as Holy Communion.
> Opportunities to plan and lead in their own worship services.
> Observation trips to see the places to which their offerings went, if near enough, also to the national Church headquarters if possible.
> More singing.
> Pageants and plays.
> Lessons that were about the Church instead of about "poor

people," because they "got that in day school." (In linking lessons with their daily experiences we had leaned too far in one direction.)

A Day of Prayer "like the women."

To know why and how the priest does certain things in the services (this from the unconfirmed), and why he wears different robes and what they mean.

To know what the creed means.

To know more about the Church building (its symbolism).

To know how religion explains science (older pupils).

To know about death and the life to come (all ages).

To have a Church School newspaper for reporting the council plans because they found too little time in the class sessions.

To have some missionaries tell about their work.

To invite the children, where special offerings went, to a party and to go and see where they worked and worshipped.

To allow each class to have the planning and leading of at least one school service a year.

To be allowed to plan and run their own parties and dances.

To know the amounts and uses made of their offerings towards Church upkeep and supplies, and to mimeograph a report of these and of the school activities to send to parents at commencement. To be allowed a vote through the council for the use of all the money given for "others."

To have more slides and films.

To have a girls' society (the boys had all the groups).

To have a representative of the council on the parish council to represent the boys and girls.

To have a summer offering and summer worship suggestions for boys and girls to use at home or at camp.

To send more young people to summer conferences. (Sixteen went at the end of the year. The offerings paid for several; the vestry paid for the others when they heard of the need. All delegates gave reports at the main morning services to the congregation the following September and October, thus bringing inspiration to the adults, also.)

In addition to these and other activities which grew out of these suggestions, every part of the Church School life was discussed and evaluated from the standpoint of boys and girls. A cartoon of the organist running with an alarm clock, ended his frequent tardiness with a friendly laugh. A cartoon of a puzzled face signified what happened to the secretary when attendance books were left unmarked. The pupils demanded our best from all of us—and got it with pleasure.

2. A MIMEOGRAPH BECOMES A JUNIOR MISSIONARY

A regular monthly bulletin was one of the first activities the council voted. It was needed to publicize plans and win co-operation. This bulletin was mailed by the boys and girls to every family. They decided that some pupils might lose it on the way home. Mailing also avoided duplication and waste of paper where several attended from one family. The machine used was an old secondhand portable which was purchased for fifteen dollars. The mimeoscope for tracing and drawing illustrations was homemade. We almost lost our minds training boys and girls to use the mimeograph and to draw their own cartoons. We were all well inked, but cleaner fluid helped that, and we gradually learned that ink was expensive and belonged on the mimeograph and not on us. This was an effort well worth the time spent in the beginning. The young people were proud of being printers; they suggested more efficient and attractive ways of using news, and often devoted their talents for office work to free the parish secretary for other jobs. It paid in many ways and developed latent talents.

Many of their council projects would have been hindered without the mimeographed bulletin. Also, class work would have suffered if all reporting had needed to be done in class time on Sundays. It more than paid for the expense in increased pupil and parent interest and in the resulting increased offerings throughout the school.

The first issue of the *Council Courier* was a great event. Vol. I—No. 1 was three pages long and set up in columns (their decision) like a newspaper. It was a pre-Lenten issue and contained headings such as: "New Quarters Become Need of Scout Troop," "Students Make Final Plans for Carnival," "Dramatic Club Formed and Will Hold Try-outs," "Seventh-grade Girls Entertained," "*Council Courier* Staff," "Editorial Board," "Support Our Missionary Magazine," "Teachers, Officers Approve New Student Undertaking," "See Our Dramatic Coach in a Play," "Feeding Time at the Zoo" (a humorous write-up on how the older boys' class noise annoyed the older girls' class nearby), "Girls Plan Leaflet" (a devotional leaflet for Lent), "Minutes of the Council Meeting," "Attendance Honor List for the First Term." Other issues grew in interest and became worldwide with mission news items. When classes began the preparation for their worship services and projects, the knowledge that their efforts would have publicity and greater usefulness through the mimeograph, increased the zeal. The mimeograph became a very important missionary asset as it ran off monthly parents' letters, worship outlines for each week, dance tickets to earn money for equipment, etc. But the machine would have lacked its usefulness without the young people who were trained (some only fourth-graders) to use it for the service to God, and they used it faithfully and well.

3. OBSERVATION TRIPS

When the *Council Courier* advertised the need for cars and parent drivers for desired observation trips, the parents seemed as eager to go as the boys and girls. We never lacked for transportation. This, too, became parent education through the boys and girls. The trips were planned monthly, and connected usually with some definite school offering or activity. Worship interest was always included and often decided the destination. "Come and see" grew out of their questioning as to "why" and "where."

Each month two members—one a council representative —were elected from and by each class. It meant disappointment for the others at times, but the trips were shared quite fairly and justly. Problems of class discipline became more rare as the council made its choices merit election. The boys and girls judged themselves and showed no apparent injustice.

It was a proud group who visited the Church headquarters and received praise for their Church School bulletin from the head of the publicity division. He had received copies by mail each month from the editors.

There was even more pride and pleasure on their faces when they went to the noonday service and found that it was the Litany service that day. They had just planned and led a Litany procession in their own Church School service, according to the old historical ritual. They knew the history of early litanies and felt a unity with their Church headquarters which no teaching in class could have given them.

After a picnic lunch (each brought his own) in Central Park, for relaxation, there was an observation trip to the

Cathedral of St. John the Divine which awed and thrilled them. One boy said, "It sits right on the top of New York, doesn't it?" Another boy shocked the guide by stealing away to sit in the Bishop's Chair. His explanation of why was enlightening—"I want to be a bishop some day and I wondered what it would feel like." The guide was instantly his friend and told us many extra things and graciously answered all our questions about the Cathedral.

After another trip to the diocesan orphanage a fourth-grade boy wrote as follows for the *Council Courier*:

On March 25th the pupils visited the Orphans' Home and took some candy and gifts. The Superintendent kindly showed us the nice cheery rooms. We saw where the children sleep, the busy kitchen, the play rooms and garden, and the laundry in the basement. There are two departments for the children, one for the girls and one for the boys. There are seventy-four children living in the home. We liked it very much. We wish more of the pupils could have gone with us and we thank the parents who loaned their cars.

The pupils went to the diocesan choir festival and saw and experienced the value of good music in worship. They visited a struggling mission to which their Advent Offering had gone, and realized that worship was present in other places and not only in a beautiful building like their own. They visited churches of other faiths and realized that worship was not limited to their own Church.

Probably these trips contributed to the wide variety of worship programs which they eventually requested and planned. The trips were required reporting to the class group and to the school bulletin. This reporting made the class lessons rather flexible and sometimes uncertain because of the after-discussion. But the teachers realized the value of these oral impressions and they co-operated. However, to overcome the lack of basic knowledge which might have resulted, the pupils, through their council, agreed to a testing plan. A certain amount of Church factual knowledge was required of each grade. An examination was given twice a year. This was done on the honor system at home. Questions were mimeographed and submitted to the teachers for approval. Then they were mailed out to the homes. The pupils could ask questions of anyone for two weeks. After that, they were on their honor to stop questioning, look at no notes, write their answers from memory, and mail or bring the answers in. Those who passed received certificates at special services. They received them proudly, and there was no apparent resentment about the exams, only disappointment felt by those who did not take much trouble the first time.

These exams also caused religion to become adult community conversation. Many telephone calls came from parents unable to answer their children's questions but wanting to do so. This fostered the value and need of a parish loan library. The pupils helped to mimeograph lists, by topics, of available books, and to mail these lists to every home. The books became mental observation trips to mission lands and to other groups in the Church family circles. Without the lists the books would have lacked much of their usefulness. For instance, a mother whose child was playing with another child who had been trained in different beliefs about the Bible, came in to find a book on the list which answered her questions. The mother of a child exposed to death for the first time came in to borrow two other books. Teachers found what they needed when the inevitable class questionings about worship came. All these preliminaries seemed an essential part of the growing interest in worship as part of all life. They were not separate steps toward it, but things which developed together as needs became apparent.

4. THE WORSHIP SCHEDULE

The new interest in worship showed itself again when the Church School time-schedule was discussed. It was unanimously voted that the worship time could not be shortened in favor of more class time for council discussion. The class session also began to seem too brief for everything the pupils wanted to do, instead of too long to endure. The "unholy rush" at the close of the services of worship solved itself into orderly marching out to a hymn, when, otherwise, it meant that their own worship plans might be made less effective. The services became theirs, not ours, and that created self-discipline. The younger pupils were being told the meaning of simple acts of worship to make the monthly invitations to the special services more valuable to them also. One small boy, when asked what he thought a Christian was, replied "A boy who gets kicked in Church and doesn't kick back." It had happened to him the Sunday before as he knelt between another boy and the teacher. The teacher explained that the other boy had been absent on the Sunday when they had learned that you close your eyes to shut out the sight of things which might take your thoughts away from God, that you put your hands together to help them to help each other not to hinder other people's worship, and the same with your feet, and that it took a strong Christian to keep them that way.

The altar for the primary department was in a large room, used by the choir for its rehearsals. But it was no longer the parking place it had been for choir boys' caps and books. The boys, themselves, reminded those who did not belong to the Church School that it was not for that purpose. A persistent offender soon found himself unpopular. It had become "our" altar and sacred to worship as it was meant to be.

As the plans for the worship services, created by the pupils, were discussed, each class was assigned its dates by the council. Every plan was submitted to the Rector for his approval at least two weeks before the date, to allow for any necessary changes. One plan brought the Rector beaming into the parish office with the statement, "At last I have found the prayer I have been looking for all my life." A typographical error had listed it as "Prayer for All Sorts and Conditions of Me." Once, when the traditional order of a service seemed reversed by a group, the Rector's question as to why, brought us a reason we deeply respected. The group had placed the General Confession at the close of a pageant. The reason given was, "We hope the pageant will make the congregation want to confess their sins." Needless to say, the plan was not altered. No plan seemed to need alteration. When questioned, the committees always had good reasons for their choices, reasons adults might have missed, but which the boys and girls saw clearly and hopefully.

Probably some of our best teacher-training was done in preparing the teachers to understand how to guide, but not limit or force, his or her own opinions on the class's planning of its chosen worship service. They were to go seeking together without embarrassment about any lack of knowledge. The teachers were free to ask for information or to appoint a class member to ask. Their main task was to be honest, open-minded, and sympathetic. Because we trusted the teachers they were trustworthy. Each knew that special help was available if requested, and the only sin was to pretend or compromise from false pride about knowledge he or she lacked. As we worked with the boys and girls we realized more and more that complete honesty is necessary to real worship.

Each class used its worship plans as a unit of study until they were completed, discussing the hymns, prayers, history, assignments of leadership for the prayers, Bible readings, and talks chosen to inform the rest of the school about the origin of some services, etc.

The seasons and special events of the year were considered in the planning. The classes studying the life of Christ, undertook the Easter service and one other. The classes learning about the Christian seasons, planned the Christmas service and one other. The class studying Church history, planned the Whitsunday service as the birthday of the Church. Classes studying missions, planned the Lenten services when the special emphasis was on the missionary offering. A class studying the Prayer Book, planned a Litany service. An older class helped to create instructions for the school services of Holy Communion.

The mechanics of the service, such as ushering, receiving the offerings, finding the places in the books and marking them, were all the responsibilities of the class in charge.

Weeks of preparation went into each service as selections were made, votes taken, and meanings discussed. After their plans were approved by the Rector, another requirement was made. Those speaking were required to come for a personal conference and trial rehearsal the day before. These were individual conferences for interpretation. They were always begun by a suggestion that, as God speaks through us in services, we are His partners, and He would like to help us to inspire others if we take time to ask Him. The director and the pupil then knelt silently for a short period of prayer for each other and for the work to be done. One small boy's response was, "Gee, I didn't know you could do that!" There was never any embarrassment because no others were present. The director then called attention to the need of thinking of that partnership in order to gain calmness and enough voice to use in this kind of serving. She explained that it was also important to know the meaning of what you were reading or saying so that the hearers would feel it too. When the pupils sensed the idea of a mission and a message, there was very little need to stress volume during the trial reading. The director retired to the rear of the church, after telling the reader that she could move forward, but not interrupt, if she could not hear clearly. This made the readers realize how important their voices were in influencing people. It made them ready to listen and learn from a brief instruction about deep breathing (a deep breath three times) before beginning, how this overcame nervousness and shortness of breath, and how they needed to read slowly with pauses for meaning and emphasis.

At one of the services a young and very shy girl discovered that an Altar Guild member had, unknown to us, changed the Bible marker to the place for the later service. The girl looked very distressed as she vainly searched for her place while the service waited. Then, just as someone was going forward to help her, she lifted her head and her voice came out strong and sure in the correct passage. She had memorized it, and prayer to her Partner had given her courage to face the ordeal. That was a turning point in the girl's life from shy awkwardness to self-confident serenity.

One class discovered that certain hymns they wanted were unsatisfactory in some verses, as they discussed the meaning. The teaching was of an outworn theology like heaven being up in the sky instead of all around us. The pupils went to work and created some verses of their own. From this creative writing the Rector and teacher discovered some of the pupils' spiritual and human hungers. One beautiful verse about the Fatherhood of God came from a shy girl to whom divorce had denied human fathering. Other members created prayers which were also enlightening to all of us. We were discovering spiritual capacities for understanding, also great needs, that we could not otherwise have realized nor filled.

Some of the following program extended into the next school year because the worship need was not discovered as a challenge until part of the first year was gone. We, like many other leaders, were too busy with the physical details to realize the riches that were escaping ourselves and our boys and girls by the superimposing of our ideas of what they needed, when they themselves knew so much more and had the capacity for seeking it, with God as their Partner.

Each of these special services will be discussed in detail for those wishing to explore them in their own way with boys and girls. However, a listing of them together as a worship calendar may prove helpful in making choices.

A Church School Calendar of Worship

DEDICATION SUNDAY—pupils, teachers, parents, and friends dedicating themselves to the work of the Church School for the year.

LITANY PROCESSION—the dramatized story of the war and harvest litanies of the early Church.

A THANKSGIVING SERVICE—the giving of food gifts to share thankfulness.

CHRISTMAS PAGEANT AND SERVICE—the giving of gifts.

EPIPHANY FESTIVAL OF LIGHTS—with a missionary emphasis.

A DAY OF PRAYER—requested after the women held one.

PRE-LENTEN MISSIONARY SERVICE—dedication and giving out of offering boxes.

WEEKLY MISSIONARY SERVICES—during Lent.

A CHURCH SCHOOL COMMUNION—a meditation on its special importance and teaching. (The service was used more frequently.)

EASTER SERVICE AND PAGEANT—presentation of the offering.

ROGATION SERVICE WITH LITANY PROCESSION—for the seedtime blessing ("Beating of the Bounds").

WHITSUNDAY SERVICE—the Birthday Thank Offering.

COMMENCEMENT SERVICE—expressions from the pupils about the year's opportunities.

SUMMER HOME WORSHIP SUGGESTIONS—to use wherever home is.

These were special services. The weekly services gave more opportunity for experiments. One older boys' class, two of whom were musicians, chose to have a musical service of meditation. This was entirely their own idea and was beautifully planned. Part of the service was without words. The pupils were asked by the leader to kneel in silent prayer while a boy played his cello. Discussion of plans revealed to the class that hymns could convey different kinds of worship. Some were sung kneeling as prayers. It was one of the most effective services.

A box of gifts was sent in October to a rural mission. This was used as the focal point for a missionary service with a talk on the Church's work in that field. The talk was given before the gifts were requested. The reason for this was to inspire interest and to cause more pleasure in the giving. The council took charge of the packing and sending of the gifts.

During Advent, before Christmas, it was the custom to give a Church School offering to a district or diocesan project. In October, the council organized an observation trip, using the volunteer parents auto corps. As a result of the trip the pupils decided that we should be praying for all the diocese with our parish as part of it, and that prayers would increase interest in the offering.

One class took over the compiling of a leaflet of intercessions. They studied the area, the needs, the kinds of people our Church should be helping, the diocesan clergy and helpers, and they also learned about their bishop. One child said, "I don't know him. Why should I pray for Him?" He was soon instructed by the other pupils. A visit from the Bishop helped the prayers to have reality and personal interest.

From their study the class made a list of people for whom to pray. One outstanding point in this discussion of the list was the subject of people in prison. Their decision was that they also needed to pray for the people who caused others to do wrong. Again they were seeing clearly to the roots of things.

Members of the class were assigned to choose suitable prayers and hymns for each need. The class voted for their final choices and assigned a class committee to compile and mimeograph the leaflet. Another committee was assigned to mail it to every Church school home for home use. A class member was appointed to tell the school about these needs at a service, urging them to use the leaflet and to give offerings.

Other spiritual gains from this leaflet were the class discussions of the meanings of chosen Bible readings and prayers and hymns. This required wise choices and they made them. Adults, by choosing for them, had been denying them this spiritual seeking and worship reality. (See page 35 for a copy of "Intercessions for Our Parish and Our Diocese," as compiled by the Church School class.)

A ninth-grade girls' class asked the director to give an illustrated lecture on her former rural work. It was scheduled for a Sunday in the spring. The pupils had learned that their Sunday was near the so-called Rogation Sunday when prayers are offered for God's blessing on the seedtime. Their prayers and hymns and readings were grouped around this theme.

The class which was assigned Palm Sunday read the story of our Lord riding into Jerusalem, and chose their theme from that. As they needed more people than their class members, they called for volunteers to portray the children of Jerusalem—boys and girls. The parents helped to prepare simple squares of colored cloth with holes cut in for their heads to go through, and pins to hold the sides together and the sashes on. This made easy costuming to wear over regular clothes. It was decided, with the Rector's approval, to hold the colorful procession at the adult service, which meant that costuming must be done quickly between sessions.

The preparation for this service was begun two weeks ahead by a talk about the story. The pupils were reminded of their opportunity to recall this story to the people of today. The need to give happy loyal service and praise was stressed when other interests tempted them to be disloyal and to hurt their Lord's cause.

The service was planned to help the congregation feel the message. The pupils who were to be in the procession were reminded that such things as whispering, tickling each other with the palms, and forgetting which place to occupy, would distract the congregation from the message. (This was suggesting trouble, but it seemed wiser, because of the larger service, not to leave these unsaid, especially when this experience of self-control might be consecrated to the service of God. This proved to be a wise decision because of the fine way in which all the pupils then co-operated.)

Two ten-minute rehearsals on two Sundays were all that were necessary. The only confusion was at the last minute when two small boys felt hurt at being omitted and wanted costumes. They were included and put in charge of a guide after they had been given hurried instructions.

The costumed boys and girls (one for each pew on each side of the center aisle of the Church) proceeded solemnly down the center aisle ahead of the choir. Each pupil stopped at his or her designated pew, turned and held a strip of palm to form an archway with the one across the aisle. At the close of the processional hymn the palms were laid quietly on the floor and the boys and girls took part in the service. The hymn before the sermon was their recessional. They quietly recovered their palms and processed out to the parish house to remove their costumes. After that, those who wished were free to return to the back of the church and, taking seats reserved for them, to continue the service. This service became an annual event for the congregation.

Whenever Baptismal or Confirmation services were held, the pupils learned about the meaning and history of these services and were urged to attend and to welcome and pray for the candidates. The smallest members felt important.

There were extra opportunities such as singing to the "shut-ins" at Christmas, planning and helping with the service for the pre-school children and babies in the spring, and serving and helping with services of their youth organizations. Especially revealing were the prayers they created for their council and other meetings and services. Not all the Sunday services were full of initiative but the fact that they were leading and planning made up for that lack to the boys and girls of the school. It was now *their* service and they had a pride and joy in it such as they had never had before.

II. PLANNING SERVICES OF DEDICATION AND THANKSGIVING AND INTERCESSION LEAFLETS

1. DEDICATION SUNDAY

This service rightfully belongs in September or early October, and so it is listed first in describing the special monthly services and in telling how they were created and conducted. However, in following through this kind of experimentation in worship, it would be a superimposed service if used the first year. The pupils would not yet have seen the need for it. They would feel, probably, that it had grown out of your desire rather than theirs. They would probably be right in thinking this. It would be more profitable for the pupils spiritually if it were a possibility brought to their attention for discussion at the end of the school year. They would be thinking ahead then to next year's school needs. The parents, teachers, staff, and pupils would seem to them more of a unit after months of tested co-operation.

Originally, this special service came up as a request from a teacher. She had seen a copy of such a service in a magazine and liked the thought of it as helpful to her own work. It was suggested at our teachers' meeting that the idea should be presented to the student council for their consideration. They liked the idea too.

As most of the service was for the adults of the Church

School, the pupils decided to leave the compiling of that part to the adults and to the Rector. The part they discussed was the one for the pupils. This was altered to fit their suggestions, and the prayer of the Confirmation Service of the Episcopal Church was used. This was suggested by those who had been confirmed as a renewal of their vows. The discussion gave them the meaning of the word "vow." It also gave them a sense of such a vow's responsibility and the need for sincerity in a contract, especially a contract with God as a Partner. Those who were confirmed profited by the review of the service's meaning which it was necessary to give to the unconfirmed members of the council.

The placing of the name of the Church in the script made it much more personal for everyone. Thus, while not a complete creation of the pupils, this service was made personal and creative as each one reverently co-operated. There was a mutual value in each group's having its own special dedication to the life of the school. Those who watched and those who promised gained in the sharing, we felt sure. There was a quiet watchfulness and reverence, even though the children turned to look at each group as they stood up for their promises.

In a small school the effectiveness of the service might be increased by having the groups go forward to the altar rail for their special part of the service. In a larger school this going forward might detract from the reverence and perhaps cause confusion and crowding. Just standing would seem more effective.

One of the values of this service, if brought to the attention of the congregation, as this was, is the fact that each member affects the life of the others. This is done by including the "friends" of the pupils who also feel a desire to dedicate themselves to their welfare spiritually. It gives a place for the unmarried and the elderly. It also helps the young people to understand that their attitudes affect the spiritual life of younger boys and girls as "helpers" or "hinderers." Often this thought is given to young people more as a threat than as a great challenge to make themselves of importance in the world by daily actions and attitudes.

2. A SERVICE OF PERSONAL DEDICATION FOR PARENTS, TEACHERS, OFFICERS, AND PUPILS*

RECTOR: It is part of the plan of God that the richest lessons and the deepest things of life shall be passed on from those who are more mature to those who are less mature. So we have the work of teachers in the world. It is a sacred responsibility and privilege of the Church to follow in the footsteps of the supreme Teacher, Jesus Christ.

For this reason, our Church has chosen those who are to be the teachers and leaders in our Church School for the coming year. We have come together at this time to commission these people for the sacred task which they are to undertake in our name.

Those who have been chosen as *officers* will please stand.

To the holy ministry of business details and to a service of unseen faithfulness in the work of organization and management,

OFFICERS: We dedicate ourselves, O Lord.

RECTOR: To co-operation with plans and counsels for bringing in Thy kingdom,

* Adapted from the *International Journal of Religious Education.*

OFFICERS: We dedicate ourselves, O Lord.

RECTOR: In the spirit and presence of Christ, do you pledge to the fulfillment of these sacred obligations the utmost of your hand, mind and inner self?

OFFICERS: I do.

RECTOR: Let us pray.

Direct us, O Lord, in all our doings, with Thy most gracious favor, and further us with Thy continual help; that in all our works begun, continued, and ended in Thee, we may glorify Thy holy Name, and finally, by Thy mercy, obtain everlasting life; through Jesus Christ our Lord. *Amen.*

RECTOR: Those who have been chosen as *teachers* will please stand. The officers may be seated.

For the children and youth of our Church and for their eager responsiveness to all that is good and beautiful and true,

TEACHERS: We give Thee, Lord, our hearty thanks.

RECTOR: For sympathetic insight into their inward selves, for patience to wait the full development of truth in their lives, for open-mindedness and respect of their personalities and contributions, for fellowship in seeking fresh interpretations of Christian truth and corporate living, and for a growing experience of God and His purpose,

TEACHERS: We earnestly beseech Thee, O Lord.

RECTOR: To the fulfillment of Christ's command, "Go ye therefore, and teach all nations . . ."

TEACHERS: We dedicate ourselves, O Lord.

RECTOR: In the spirit and presence of Christ, do you pledge to the fulfillment of these sacred obligations the utmost of your hand, mind and inner self?

TEACHERS: I do.

RECTOR: Let us pray.

O God, by whom the meek are guided in judgment, and light riseth up in the darkness for the godly; grant us, in all our doubts and uncertainties, the grace to ask what Thou wouldst have us to do, that the Spirit of Wisdom may save us from all false choices, and that in Thy light we may see light, and in Thy straight path may not stumble; through Jesus Christ our Lord. *Amen.*

RECTOR: The *parents and older friends of our pupils* will please stand. The teachers may be seated.

Do you in the presence of God and of each other, promise to give these chosen leaders the wholehearted co-operation in the home and elsewhere so necessary to the accomplishment of their task?

PARENTS AND FRIENDS: As the parents and friends of the pupils to whose service these teachers and leaders have now been commissioned, we pledge our loyal support, our sympathetic co-operation in the home, and our patience and goodwill in working together upon our common, sacred task.

RECTOR: Let us pray.

Almighty God, heavenly Father, who hast blessed us with the joy and care of children; Give us light and strength so to train them, that they may love whatsoever things are true and pure and lovely and of good report, following the example of their Saviour Jesus Christ. *Amen.*

RECTOR: As your rector and leader in Christ Jesus, I hereby solemnly commission you parents, teachers, and officers to serve as fellow-workers in the high privilege of Christian education in the Church School of ——— Church.

RECTOR: Will the *pupils* of the Church School please stand. All others may be seated.

As pupils of the Church School of ——— Church and disciples of Jesus Christ our Lord, will you serve Him by faithfully trying to live in His way in your homes, in your community, in your school, and in your Church as you promised, or was promised for you, at your Baptism?

PUPILS: I will by God's help.

RECTOR: Let us pray.

Defend, O Lord, these Thy children with Thy heavenly grace; that they may continue Thine for ever; and daily increase in Thy Holy Spirit more and more, until they come into Thine everlasting kingdom. *Amen.*

RECTOR: Let us all rise and pledge our loyalty to Christ and to His Church by repeating the Creed. (*All rise*)

RECTOR AND CONGREGATION: (The Creed)

RECTOR: "Not everyone that saith unto me, Lord, Lord, shall enter into the kingdom of heaven; but he that doeth the will of my Father which is in heaven."

OFFERTORY: Hymn ———.

DOXOLOGY.

CLOSING PRAYERS: The Lord's Prayer.
            Church School Prayer. (*All in unison*)

O Heavenly Father, bless, we beseech Thee, the pupils, teachers, and officers, the parents and friends of the Church School. Give vision and inspiration to all who are to teach. Grant unto us as pupils that we may increase in obedience, loyalty, and love to Thy Son Jesus Christ. May we remember to keep our lips pure, and that the body is the temple of the Holy Ghost. In our homes, may we give love and obedience to our parents. In our Church, may we be reverent and devout. In our school, may we be studious, fair in play, and friendly with one another. For our country, may we be ready to sacrifice and to serve, through Thy Son, our Saviour, Jesus Christ. *Amen.*

PRAYER FOR RELIGIOUS EDUCATION.

BENEDICTION.

RECESSIONAL HYMN.

3. A LITANY PROCESSION

In going through the Church Prayer Book one class discovered and decided on the Litany Service as their choice. Inevitably, they asked questions about where it came from. They were given a book in the library called *The Romance of the Book of Common Prayer* by Burgess, a source which was frequently very helpful to the council and the teachers.

They became so interested in the story of the first litanies, the torchlight processions in ancient Rome in time of battle and siege, the Rogation litanies at the time of planting and harvest, and the fact that this was the first of their own Prayer Book services translated into English, that they wanted to tell the whole school about all these things. They asked if they could first tell the stories and then have the service in procession as originally intended. The staff kept their fingers crossed as they wondered what mischievous boys might do to such a procession. The Rector approved, and we trusted this class as we had trusted the others, only with more misgivings.

They were given the opportunity to lead. However, they requested the Rector to say the prayers "as the bishops did in Rome." One of the class members told the stories after the opening hymn. This was an advantage. He sensed every bit of adventure, and won the interest of the congregation of boys and girls as a grown-up might not have done.

Another member of the class explained the mechanics of the service. He instructed the classes to stand still with heads bowed and eyes closed for the prayers or petitions, and to march forward as they made the responses after each petition, pausing for the next petition. At the close of the petitions they were to pause again for the blessing. Then there would be a hymn, during which they were to file back into their pews.

When the time came for the procession, the Rector, followed by the choir, came down from the chancel and started down the center aisle. The pupils fell into line, two by two. It was a fine opportunity for old-time pushing and giggling. We rather expected it from pure nervousness and excitement. We were ashamed at our lack of faith when we realized the solemnity and reverence they were giving instead. They were pilgrims and soldiers marching the torchlit streets of ancient Rome. You could see it in their uplifted faces as they marched round the aisles to each response and paused with bowed heads and closed eyes for the prayers. There was no disorder as they filed back into their pews, singing the hymn. It was a religious experience for all of us.

In evaluating the service afterwards a criticism came up. The words were too grown-up for the younger members. Could they create their own litanies, perhaps a peace litany for the Sunday nearest Memorial Day? They submitted a fine simple outline and the Rector approved it. This taught them that, though forms were helpful, they were not required always to abide by the original wording even in the Episcopal Church.

Little children, especially, like litanies because of the repetition in the responses. After these two services the hymn litanies became more meaningful and were chosen often. One three-lined one with seventeen verses which ends each verse with "Hear us, Holy Jesus," was often used in sections for meaning.

4. A THANKSGIVING SERVICE

It was at Thanksgiving that we discovered that the pupils were rather fed up with the usual way of "giving baskets to the poor" because they "got that in day school."

Not wanting them to be fed up with the idea of sharing or sympathy or thankfulness, nor to feel snobbish or shrinking according to their financial privileges, we realized that a spiritual need had been neglected. As the season drew near the teachers were warned of the dangers in their teaching. It was decided to base the teaching on worship—to give out information about ancient thanksgiving services, and to lead up to present-day situations and plans.

The pupils were told of the old heathen festivals and of the often cruel rituals with sacrifices of human life. This gave them a contrast with the apparent safety of their own day—one cause for thankfulness to God.

This, in turn, brought out the story of Abraham and his discovery that God did not want human sacrifice. From that came the stories of the offering of harvested food, the offering of doves and lambs in Jesus' time on earth, the difference between offering these gifts as ritualistic habits or as worship. The story of Cain's jealousy of Abel showed the wrong kind of offering spirit. Attitudes began to seem important and personal—something they could understand. "Giving baskets to the poor" began to have a meaning of thankfulness for their own good fortune and a desire that others might have it too. God wanted them to share in thankfulness for those who had shared with them—their parents, the family earners, the workers.

The lists of simple blessings made by the pupils then had

a richer meaning. The prayers they created were more real and sincere and were their own, not something we expected of them or God expected of them. They began to sense that thankfulness was a gift for each day, not a required one-day-a-year ritual and eating feast.

The council members were told of the old Church harvest festivals of England. They decided on this type of service and instructed the class members to bring gifts of food insofar as they were able. These were taken to the altar rail during the simple thanksgiving service and piled on the altar steps, to symbolize that the Owner and Creator of all life was the One who should receive the gifts before they were distributed to those who needed them.

The service was held on the Sunday before Thanksgiving Day since a community service was planned for Thanksgiving Day itself. There seemed to be joy in the giving instead of boredom, and we felt that the gifts were "given in His Name." The pupils were told that one potato was enough if that was all they could bring, that the thankfulness and sharing with the gift was the important part, and that God understood if their gift was sincere. The gifts were divided into portions and taken by a girls' group to those needing them. The places chosen were institutions and the offices of a local society which promised to redistribute them to families. It seemed wiser not to embarrass the families themselves. Some of the personal contact was lost in this way, but the council members, when approached as to how the families would feel, decided the impersonal way was more kind to the receivers. In this way they had the spiritual value of trying to feel the emotions of the receiver.

5. INTERCESSIONS FOR OUR PARISH AND OUR DIOCESE*

We may talk to God as naturally as we talk to our closest friends, but we often find it hard to say what we most deeply feel. Use these suggested prayers and the books of prayer as guides, stopping whenever you feel the desire to talk with God in your own thoughts and words, or to listen with a free mind for helpful thoughts from Him. If thoughts come about ways in which our school could serve those for whom we are praying, have the high courage to share them afterwards with your Rector, your teacher, or your class, as Christ's faithful soldier and servant. God may want to speak through you to us. No one is too young to be His messenger and helper. (This section was contributed on request by an adult.)

"Closer is He than breathing—nearer than hands and feet."

> O God unseen yet ever near,
> Thy presence may we feel;
> And thus inspired with holy fear,
> Before thine altar kneel. *Amen.*

"This is my commandment, That ye love one another, as I have loved you."

"He that hath my commandments, and keepeth them, he it is that loveth me: and he that loveth me shall be loved of my Father, and I will love him, and will make myself known to him."

"Our prayers are like raindrops flowing together to do great

---

* See page 21 for description of how this leaflet of intercessions was compiled by the pupils.

deeds, like a mighty river giving power and growing life far from where the raindrops fell."

> As torrents in the summer
> Half dried in their channels,
> Suddenly rise, though the
> Sky is still cloudless,
> For rain has been falling
> Far off at their fountains:
>
> So hearts that are fainting
> Grow full to o'erflowing,
> And they that behold it
> Marvel, and know not
> That God at their fountains
> Far off has been raining!

Let us think of the sick people in our parish and in the hospitals of our diocese.

Let us think of the sick people who are alone and neglected because we who belong to the Church have not tried hard enough to find and help them.

Let us think especially of the little children who are puzzled and frightened by illness and do not know how to help themselves.

Let us help them by our prayers—

O God, the strength of the weak and the comfort of sufferers; mercifully accept our prayers, and grant to Thy sick servants, for whom we pray, the help of Thy healing power, that their sickness may be turned into health, and their sorrow into joy; through Jesus Christ our Lord. *Amen.*

Let us think of the doctors, nurses, chaplains, our Rector, and all who minister to the sick—

Almighty Father, teach Thy servants to pray so faithfully that they may be drawn near to Thee and learn Thy will. Help them to serve so joyfully that others may be drawn to Thee. May Thy Holy Spirit guide them each day, that all they think or say or do may be acceptable in Thy sight. We ask all for the sake of Him who taught us that healing the sick is part of the Church's work upon earth, our Saviour Jesus Christ. *Amen.*

"The prayer of faith shall save the sick."

Let us pray that we may help others to overcome their illnesses, sins, and troubles, as Jesus did, through deepening and strengthening our own faith by prayer—

> O fill me with thy fullness, Lord,
> Until my very heart o'erflow
> In kindling thought and glowing word,
> Thy love to tell, thy praise to show.

Let us think of those who are in the prisons and jails of our diocese. Some are innocent victims of other people's cowardice and wrong-doing. Let us pray that the weak cowards may become strong enough to take their own punishment and overcome the temptation to let others suffer in their places—

O God who beholdest the hidden secrets of our hearts, help us all to be honest in Thy sight and before all men. Make us sincere in word and deed. May we not wish to profit by what would rob others, but may they be safe with us. Above all may we not tempt others to dishonesty in word or deed. Give us the courage to endure injustice from others with calm trust and strength and a clear conscience, as our Leader, Jesus Christ, endured. *Amen.*

Some have become law-breakers because others tempted them to think that the easy, selfish thing was brave, forgetting that it takes a strong, unselfish character to keep the law. A patriot keeps the laws of his country and a Christian patriot keeps the laws of God and his country.

"Watch and pray, lest ye enter into temptation."

Let us pray for a clearer vision for those who are tempted to think that lack of self-control is brave—

O Jesus, our Companion, help us as we walk in Thy way; so that following Thy light we may keep the way of righteousness, and never wander away into darkness and confusion of the world's false light while Thou who art the Way, the Truth, and the Life art shining within us. *Amen.*

Some are in prison because of the injustices of our living conditions. They never had a chance to know the right way. Let us pray for honest government and for honest work and fair play for all people—

Loving Father, make us, and all members of our Church, ready to do our part as Christian citizens in building an honest government for our country, and in improving living conditions for all who live in our land and in other lands. Teach us to be useful to others in Christ's way; to feel for the poor and suffering; and to be ready to serve all who are in need; for Jesus' sake. *Amen.*

Some are in prison because they felt they had no one to care for them or to help them.

Let us think of the chaplains of our Church who are visiting those prisoners who are lonely and bitter and in need of Christian friendship—

> Father, who on man dost shower,
>   Gifts of plenty from thy dower,
> To thy people give the power
>   All thy gifts to use aright.
>
> Give pure happiness in leisure,
>   Temperance in every pleasure,
> Holy use of earthly treasure,
>   Bodies clear and spirits bright.

Lift from this and every nation
  All that brings us degradation;
Quell the forces of temptation;
  Put thine enemies to flight.

Be with us, thy strength supplying,
  That with energy undying,
Every foe of man defying,
  We may rally to the fight.

Thou who art our Captain ever
  Lead us on to great endeavor;
May thy Church the world deliver,
  Give us wisdom, courage, might. *Amen.*

Let us think of those who are in our diocesan Church homes
—the old people, the children who have no fathers and
mothers, the little babies whose mothers have no homes
for them—

Lord Jesus, the great Comforter, help us through Thy Church
to give Thy comfort, light and peace to all who are in need or
in any ways afflicted in mind, body or soul; Help us to comfort
them with friendliness given in Thy Name and for Thy sake
as members of Thy family. *Amen.*

"Pray ye therefore the Lord of the harvest that he will send
forth laborers into his harvest."

"Also I heard the voice of the Lord, saying, Whom shall I
send, and who will go for us? Then said I, Here am I; send
me."

Let us think of those who have answered God's call and are
serving in our diocese—

O heavenly Father, we thank Thee for all who have heard
Thy call and gone forth to sacrifice and to serve in Thy Name.

Grant them joy in Thy service; courage in hard things; patience in discouragement; love in their serving; and the peace and strength of Thy Presence each day; through Jesus Christ our Lord. *Amen*.

"Inasmuch as ye have done it unto one of the least of these, my brethren, ye have done it unto me."

"No man hath seen God at any time. If we love one another, God dwelleth in us, and His love is perfected in us."
Let us pray for ourselves, thinking of what we want to do with our lives, and asking God to guide us to make right choices—

Lord Jesus, who came into the world not to be served, but to serve, give me, I pray Thee, the spirit of service. Help me to seek not my own good only but also the good of others. Show me how to help those who are near to me. Make me considerate of the weak, the aged and the unfortunate. Show me what I can do for them. If I can bear their burdens make me glad to do it. Teach me that a heart that seeks to do good to others has more happiness than a heart that seeks only its own pleasures. By unselfish service may I learn that it is more blessed to give than to receive. For Thine own sake we ask it. *Amen*.

O Saviour of the world, bless those who are in training for the work of Thy Church, and help me when the time comes for me to decide my life work to remember this service as a way of life to which I have been called in Baptism. Keep me ready and willing to answer that call, and guide me to serve Thee in whatever task I undertake, for Thy sake who dared to give all and count it joy for love of us. *Amen*.

"You have not chosen me, but I have chosen you and appointed you to go and bring forth fruit."

"Lo, I am with you alway, even unto the end of the world."

III. OBSERVING CHRISTMAS AND THE EPIPHANY

1. CREATING A CHRISTMAS PAGEANT

All the classes united for a Christmas pageant, but one older class was in charge. Several possibilities were discussed by the council. The one decided upon was an idea from another place where one of the teachers had woven a pageant around the idea of Saint Nicholas's story (see page 44). The council had no copy, only the idea. Based on this, they wrote their own words, designed pantomimes, and selected a musical service.

They requested the Rector to be a combination bishop, Santa Claus, and reader. His vestments were so like both phases of the character (bishop and Santa Claus) that one of the smallest children reached out and patted his red cloak as he processed down the center aisle to the litany desk. There, after introductory music, he told the Christmas legend of Saint Nicholas of Myra. Then he called his groups of Christmas symbols, group by group, to do homage to the Christ Child.

There was much discussion about getting the groups into position without confusion as they gradually formed into a beautiful setting. Before the service the manger was placed on the step at the opening of the altar rail. That, and the Christmas decorations of the church, were the only stage settings for the pageant. A low covered seat was placed beside the manger for Mary.

There were more requests for adult guidance and help with this pageant than with the Easter one. By then, the pupils had more confidence and had had the experience of this and of other dramatics.

The carolers were chosen to enter first to form a choir. They were robed in old English costumes and processed singing, to take their places in the choir stalls. As they entered, Mary and Joseph walked slowly in, Joseph helping Mary, to take their position by the manger. Mary gently raised the covering, revealing a glowing light in the manger to symbolize the Christ Child.

Following in order the call of Saint Nicholas, each singing a special carol, came the evergreens with their wreaths, the candles with their lights, the bells ringing out a merry jingle, and the little Christmas trees who walked very sedately to avoid spilling their sprinkled star dust.

As each group approached the manger, they knelt and presented their Advent offerings of money and their gifts of toys. Then they took their position in the growing tableau.

When all were in place, Saint Nicholas reached out into the middle aisle to take the smallest children near him by the hand. He then called for all the pupils and the congregation to process to the manger to offer their loving hearts and their offerings to the Christ Child. Everyone in the church filed in procession to the manger, and then went back to their seats while carols were sung. When all were again seated, the lights were dimmed and a small angel sang a lullaby by the manger.

A vestryman who stood in the rear of the Church said afterwards, "I have suffered through many pageants, but this I enjoyed, Why?" It was because the actors were remembering meanings and action rather than words. Even Saint

Nicholas could read his words and not be worried by long arduous memorizing at a busy season. It was the pupils' choice and they were enjoying it also, without the nerve tension of remembering words. Because they knew that the way they looked and acted was giving a message, they were concentrating on doing each action as reverently and beautifully as possible. Also, they had voted in each class for those who were to take part. This was an honor given to the actors by their classmates. However, no one who was voted for was forced to take part if it embarrassed him. The director remembered a previous pageant in another place when one boy had preferred a dose of castor oil to a part in a play. His mother, thinking to help had given him his choice. To some boys and girls acting is a torture they resent. Some in this group may have conquered that torture to give their gift to the Christ Child. It has been done, sometimes secretly, sometimes not so secretly.

The parents took care of all the entrance cues from typed instructions. The groups had been rehearsed and costumed in small groups. The dress rehearsal was the only united one. This made it easier for everyone. The nerve strain of most dramatization had been eliminated and all could enjoy the united effort. An alert parent cued the organist, thus relieving him of the tension of remembering. Everything was co-ordinated in one rehearsal. All the well-known symbols of Christmas were there with a worshipping significance, and Christmas and Santa Claus belonged wholly to the Christ Child. The pupils had their parties, too, which they planned themselves. However, I doubt whether any of those boys and girls ever forget that Santa Claus was a bishop who served God through Christmas worship and through kindness. No one doubted that there was a Santa Claus, but he ceased to be just a secular myth who later had to be discarded.

2. SAINT NICHOLAS OF MYRA: A CHRISTMAS CAROL SERVICE

PLACE: The Church, the Place of Giving.
TIME: The Birthday of our Lord, the Time of Giving.

CHARACTERS:

JOSEPH, the Guardian of the Christ Child.

MARY, the Mother of the Christ Child.

THE ANGEL, the heavenly Guardian.

BISHOP NICHOLAS OF MYRA, whom some call Saint Nicholas or Santa Claus.

THE SHEPHERDS, the first Gift Bringers.

THE WISE MEN, who bring gold and frankincense and myrrh.

THE CAROLLERS, who bring a gift of song.

THE CHRISTMAS CANDLES, who bring a gift of light.

THE CHRISTMAS EVERGREENS, who bring a gift of life and hope.

THE CHRISTMAS BELLS, who bring a gift of merry joy.

THE CHRISTMAS TREES, who bring a gift of loyalty.

THE CONGREGATION, who bring the gift of loving hearts.

SUGGESTIONS FOR PRODUCING

Staging

The church decorated for the Christmas services makes the best setting. A simple wooden manger should be placed in the chancel, in the center, outside the sanctuary rail. Two logs or low wooden stools are needed for Mary and Joseph, near the manger. The Christ Child should be represented only by a light in the manger. A large flash-light, fastened securely to a small baby pillow, wound round with white cheesecloth, to represent swaddling clothes, makes it very convenient for Mary to turn on the light as she draws back the covering when she first enters, allowing the light to shine up into her face.

Candles should be placed safely away from decorations in each of the church windows in the nave, if the windows are low enough for the candles to be lighted. These are lighted by the CANDLE BEARERS during their entrance.

Costumes

JOSEPH—Eastern dress and long cloak—a staff—sandals.

MARY—Rose pink or white robe and blue cloak.

ANGEL—Pure white—silver band for headdress.

BISHOP NICHOLAS—Priest's vestments with bishop's sleeves attached—long red cloak (circular) which trails, bordered with white imitation fur to give a resemblance to Santa Claus—bishop's mitre or crown with a high point in the front, with a headpiece of red which shows above the mitre a little to resemble Santa Claus' hat—white beard and moustache to resemble Santa Claus.

CAROLLERS—Choir in vestments, or in old English Tudor costumes.

CANDLES—Orange cheesecloth robes—tinsel bands for headdress—tinsel girdles.

EVERGREENS—Pale green and white robes—gold bands for headdress—wreaths of laurel or other evergreen hung around the neck.

BELLS—Bright red capes, knee length—red hats—both capes and hats trimmed with small tinkling bells—red slippers.

CHRISTMAS TREES—Dark green tarlatan or mosquito netting tied on the top of the head with tinsel and draped over white dresses to give a pointed effect from the top of the head to the knees—brown footwear to represent the tree trunk—a silver star tied into the top of each "tree"—silver snow scattered over all (or silver rain).

SHEPHERDS—Dark tunics or long Eastern robes—Eastern headdress and sandals.

WISE MEN—Rich Eastern robes—a king's crown, a turban, a silver band over a draped Eastern headdress for the three types of king.

Properties

GIFTS—With the exception of the WISE MEN, the gifts each character brings should be real, possibly toys for a group of children for Christmas or for any local activity that is planned for Christmas giving. The congregation as well as the cast bring gifts, some bringing money. If there is an Advent or Christmas school offering to be given, the pupils of the school may bring both that gift and a toy if they wish.

JOSEPH—A staff on which to lean during the long service.

CANDLES—Tall white or red candles. These should be lighted just before the entrance and the church window candles lighted from them by the CANDLE BEARERS. Flash-lights fixed into long, covered, mailing tubes may be used for greater safety.

EVERGREENS—Ropes of evergreen cut into strands long enough to hang gracefully on each character.

SHEPHERDS—Shepherds' crooks. These may be made from

mop handles by making a foundation top of rolled newspaper and wire shaped into the semblance of a crook and fastened securely to the stick. Wind all with strips of brown crepe paper, fastening it with strong brown thread.
Wise Men—A gold box, an incense burner, a small silver box.

Lighting

The church should be dimly lighted to give contrast to the candles in the windows. The chancel should be lighted with a bright light diffused by gold, if possible, to give contrast to the light in the manger and the light of the star. The latter should be hung over the chancel steps or directly over the altar. If possible, have an electrician attach a dimmer to the star so that it may light gradually as the Wise Men approach.

Rehearsals

If group rehearsals are held it will only be necessary to have two full rehearsals, including the dress rehearsal.

All ages may be included in the cast. The Rector may take the part of Bishop Nicholas, as his is the only speaking part. This part may be read from a scroll if desired, except for the bidding to the congregation to bring their gifts, when he must face them to be effective.

Each group's entrance may be placed in charge of different parents—each of whom should be given typed cues and directions. This will give the players more confidence than if the director tries to give all the cues; it will also leave the director free for the general details or for emergencies.

The number in the cast for each symbol may be planned

according to the space available. This service is planned with six of each to give a colorful tableau. More or fewer people may be used.

THE CAROL SERVICE

CHOIR (*Off-stage*)—Hymn, "O little town of Bethlehem—"

(*Enter* MARY *and* JOSEPH *during the second verse.* JOSEPH *stands on the far side of the manger, looking down at it, leaning on his staff.* MARY *sits beside the manger, bends over it, and slowly draws back the cover. As she does so, the light in the manger shines up into her face.*)

MARY—*Sings a lullaby to the Christ Child.*

CHOIR (*Off-stage*)—Hymn, "While shepherds watched—"

SHEPHERDS (*Enter during the singing of the first verse, going slowly forward from the rear of the church to kneel after hurrying up the chancel steps when they see the Christ Child. At the end of the hymn they go forward and place their gifts by the manger, then draw to one side.*)

CHOIR (*Off-stage*)—Hymn, "We three kings—"

WISE MEN (*Enter from the rear of the church during the first verse. As they enter the star slowly lights. They kneel and bow low in Eastern fashion on the chancel steps. As the second, third and fourth verses are sung, each, in turn, goes forward to give his gift of symbolic value and then withdraws, to stand at the opposite side from the shepherds.*)

BISHOP NICHOLAS (*Enters on the fifth verse from the rear of the church. He kneels on the top step of the chancel in homage to the Christ before saying, while still kneeling*):

O little Child of Bethlehem, I, Bishop Nicholas of Myra, whom some have called saint and whom little children, like Thyself, have known as their friend Santa Claus, long ago learned of Thy love for all men, then, through that love, of the great joy which comes from sharing with others in their need. Help us, we pray Thee, to keep that joy on the feast of Thy birth, so that all men may come to worship Thee in all things and to serve and love each other for Thy sake.

(*Rises and turns to the congregation saying*):

Listen, and you shall hear the legend of Bishop Nicholas whom you call Saint Nicholas or Santa Claus.

Long ago, on a cold winter night in a city called Myra, I heard, in a home, the sound of a young girl's weeping. Hoping to help, I listened, and heard the sad tale of a family needing food. I heard of a brave girl's willingness to provide her loved ones with food by marrying a rich man whom she feared.

Silently, I stole away and, hurrying to my store of gold, tied some in small bags. Then, with these, back to the unhappy home I went. I climbed to the roof and dropped the bags down the chimney with such a crash that it startled the people within. I rejoiced to hear the tears change to happy laughter on the Christ Child's birthday. It was such fun to change weeping to laughter that ever since on the eve of His birthday, my spirit has roamed the earth, bringing love and joy to families everywhere, when love would let me come in to make hearts glad.

(*Turning again to the manger*):

I will bring to you, O Saviour of the world, my symbols of happiness which are bringing joy to others in Thy Name.

(*Turning to the congregation*):

Come carollers! Bring us your gift of joy in song!

CHOIR (*Enter singing*)—Hymn, "Good Christian men rejoice—" (*Kneel in two's, presenting gifts at the manger and then withdrawing to the choir stalls.*)

BISHOP NICHOLAS—Draw near and shine for us, Christmas Candles, symbols of the coming of the Light of the World.

CHOIR—Hymn, "Like silver lamps in a distant shrine—"

CHRISTMAS CANDLES (*Enter with lighted candles from the rear of the church during the first verse, two going down each aisle to light the window candles. They meet at the chancel steps. The first two go to the center of the top step and kneel. The next two kneel on the second step. The third two kneel on the next step. At the end of the hymn they rise and form two slanting rows of light at the end of the choir stalls, the first two going toward the rear stall, etc.*)

BISHOP NICHOLAS—Ho! Christmas Evergreens, symbols of the everlasting and ever-growing love of your Creator! Bring us your gifts of life and hope."

CHOIR—Hymn, "It came upon the midnight clear—"

CHRISTMAS EVERGREENS (*Enter down each aisle from the rear. They kneel before the manger until the music ends, then offering their gifts and withdraw, three to each side, facing the congregation.*)

BISHOP NICHOLAS—And now, O Christmas Bells, ring out your mirth and joy and bring us your merry message of the beauty and holiness of common things when melted by the fire of love and molded together by a Master Workman, our God of Love.

CHOIR—Hymn, "All my heart this night rejoices—"

CHRISTMAS BELLS (*Enter from the rear, running merrily, two down each of the three aisles. When they meet they join hands, the first boy holding his finger to his lips for silence. They go slowly up the chancel steps on tip-toe to kneel before the manger. When the music stops they rise, offer their gifts and stand one on each of the chancel steps facing the manger.)*

BISHOP NICHOLAS—Bring us your gift of loyalty, little trees of God, symbols of Christmas joy, pointing to higher things and standing straight and true in all the storms.

CHOIR—Hymn, "Saw you never in the twilight—"

CHRISTMAS TREES—(*Enter from the rear, hand in hand, by two's. They go down the middle and side aisles, two down each. They meet and go up to kneel in the chancel until the end of the hymn. They rise, present their gifts and return down the steps to stand three on each side below where the candles stand, facing the steps.)*

BISHOP NICHOLAS—Another symbol I have to offer. It lies in the hearts of all—the spirit of giving. Come, ye children, young and old, show the world that the spirit of Santa Claus is the Spirit of the Christ Child by bringing your loving gifts for others to His manger.

Come! I will lead you to worship Him. (*He comes to the front seats and leads the children—taking the hands of two—and the congregation to the manger. There they place their gifts, returning quietly to their seats.)*

CHOIR—Hymn, "O, come all ye faithful—" (*Singing begins when* BISHOP NICHOLAS *starts to go down the aisle to lead the children. Singing is continued until all are in their places again.)*

BISHOP NICHOLAS—"All things come of Thee, and of Thine own have we given Thee." (*When all are quiet*) Hush! an angel comes to sing a lullaby to the heavenly Child. Let us all kneel for our goodnight to Him and to each other. (*Kneels*).

(*All kneel*)

ANGEL (*Enters from the sacristy while* BISHOP NICHOLAS *is speaking and stands on the kneeling cushion by the altar rail near the manger while she sings "Silent Night."*)

(*As the* ANGEL *leaves at the close of the hymn,* MARY *covers the manger and, slowly rising, goes off with* JOSEPH, *making their exit through the sacristy.*)

BISHOP NICHOLAS (*As soon as* MARY *and* JOSEPH *have left*)— The Peace of God, which passeth all understanding, keep your hearts and minds in the knowledge and love of God, and of his Son Jesus Christ our Lord: and the blessing of God Almighty, the Father, the Son, and the Holy Ghost, be amongst you, and remain with you always. *Amen.*

CHOIR—Recessional hymn, "Hark, the herald angels sing—"

(*Repeat as long as necessary until the choir is out of the church.*)

> *Order of Recessional*
> Bishop Nicholas
> Christmas Trees
> Christmas Bells
> Evergreens
> Candle Bearers
> Shepherds
> Wise Men
> Choir

(*Quiet music should be continuously played between the hymns.*)

3. EPIPHANY—THE FESTIVAL OF LIGHTS

This was an adult evening service, planned by adults. Our opportunity was to enrich it for the boys and girls and to try to give them its full meaning.

They were told the significance of the coming of light to the world through the Christ Child, and how the wise men who visited Him were the first to take that light to the gentile world. The service was described—the dark Church —the lighting of the one Christ candle by the Rector as Christ's representative to us—the four evangelists lighting their candles from the Christ candle—their coming to others with the message and the light—the gradual lighting of the candle of each member of the congregation until the church twinkled with light—the returning home from the church trying to keep each candle burning—the significance of relighting it if it blew out in the night—burning it in the home as long as possible.

The young people took part as the choir, evangelists, and prophets, also as part of the congregation. Some took the meaning so seriously that they told of staying awake until their individual candle burned entirely away—keeping vigil. These were told the story of how the knights of old kept vigil—how they knelt alone in dark churches until dawn on the eve of their knighting, testing their strength, patience and endurance by holding their swords upright. A picture of this made a deep impression, especially on the boys. The story of our Lord's vigils of prayer and of the night in Gethsemane had a deeper meaning and value. Probably, the teaching value of this service or vigil of lights was, for some, the banishing of the thought of our Lord from an effeminate atmosphere into strength.

IV. LENTEN ACTIVITIES: OFFERINGS, SERVICES, PRAYER LEAFLETS

1. LENTEN PLANS

When Christmas was over, the council discussed Lenten needs and dedicated Epiphany and Pre-Lent to preparation. They decided on four main ideas:

(1) Another prayer leaflet for Lent like the Advent one for home use. This they prepared, mimeographed, and distributed in the same way, after much discussion of form and plan. They found it hard to decide whether to have a weekly plan for the six weeks or a daily one to be repeated each week. The daily plan was decided on as best. For a copy of the leaflet, see page 63.

(2) The earning of offerings and the compiling of methods of earning through dedicating written slips in a large mite box. (A big, gold-covered one was made with gold wings. This was renamed "The Might Box." It was used on the altar each Sunday, and any boy or girl could offer his or her effort to God in writing when the leader called for the slips to be brought forward.)

(3) Special talks and services about the Church's mission during Lent. The talks were to be given by the boys or girls selected from the classes in charge of the services each Sunday.

(4) An effort to spread information about the Church's mission through soliciting parish subscriptions for the Church's missionary magazine.

The council was shown the national printed Lenten

material. They had the choice of that or of their own. They decided to use the national plan. The weekly services were assigned to different classes and they proceeded to make the printed material their own from then on.

There was an easier assignment for the younger grades. Each of these grades decided to do its own Bible readings and talks, but they requested the Rector to lead the prayers, even their own compiled ones. This was not prompted by fear of doing it, but by a desire to have it as perfect as possible and as helpful. The Rector was a partner now—a trusted one.

2. RAISING MONEY FOR THE LENTEN OFFERING

A council committee mimeographed a bulletin for parents. This suggested ways of earning and saving Lenten offerings, and was an attempt to secure parents' co-operation. The pupils knew the value of this more than we did. A talk to parents by one of the council members requested help with saving and earning rather than receiving last minute "handouts" from them. This was a surprise to the parents and a lesson for their own giving. The offerings could be earned with parental co-operation. Parents' offerings could also be given, but as their own as the adult division of the school.

Another leaflet was compiled to advertise the magazine and request subscriptions. This was compiled from excerpts from advertising literature sent out by the magazine, plus effective line drawings of their own. They were proud of the commendation the national office sent them about this. This was the write-up that pupil editors put in their *Council Courier*:

The Church School has again taken up the usual Lenten task of selling our missionary magazine to the members of the parish. Your support is needed. Remember that in becoming a subscriber you enter the missionary field yourself; and each new subscriber adds one more recruit to the Church's work. The readers are informed churchmen. They know the needs, how they are being met or not met. The sooner the magazine is placed in every home the easier it will be for the parish to meet its responsibilities.

They seemed to pick out the most vital statements in condensing news. No door-to-door canvassing for subscriptions was permitted. The pupils wanted this activity, but the parents requested them not to do it, feeling that it was unsafe for young people in that community.

The slips describing the efforts of saving and earning offerings were collected and later compiled into a list of suggestions for the next year to send to the homes. In this way the "Might Box" fulfilled two purposes—a dedication of effort (a new idea they adopted from a former national Lenten leaflet) and help for the future. The amount of the offerings each pupil gave was not known except by the treasurer since some had less opportunity than others. The *effort*, rather than the *amount*, was stressed as being important to God, but the amounts increased. It was a willing offering and not a forced one. It was an act of worship.

To advertise the mission fields weekly exhibits of curios were ordered and cared for by different classes. These were obtained from another Church's headquarters and promptly packed and returned. The primary and kindergarten departments contributed to these displays with sand-table exhibits, prepared the week before for the older pupils and parents.

About this time, the afternoon meeting of the mothers and teachers came into being, and was called "The Church School

Fellowship." They requested a discussion of the ways and teachings of the Church during Lent. The council had included in its plans a Friday afternoon worship service with a story. The Fellowship decided to worship with them, and then retire to the parish house for discussion, while the boys and girls remained in the church for their story. They all went home together afterwards. This proved to be a good worship plan for both groups, and increased the fellowship between them in the Church.

Notices of this plan had to be sent out by the council. There were mimeograph committees all over the place for a while. This letter to the parents, however, although mimeographed by the pupils, was sent out by the teachers as their contribution to the Lenten effort. In it was also the notice of a Missionary Carnival, approved by teachers and pupils, and anticipated by both as fun in earning. The plan was as follows:

Kindergarten and 1st grade—A Fishpond
2nd and 3rd grades—A Candy Shoppe
4th-grade girls—Japanese Tea Room
4th-grade boys—Indian Game Booth (pay to play)
5th-grade boys—Seamen's Soft Drink Stand
6th-grade girls—Country Grocery Store
6th-grade boys—Hawaiian Game Booth (pay to play)
7th-grade girls—Home Missions Bakery
7th-grade boys—Ellis Island Movie Theater
8th-grade girls—African White Elephant Gift Shop
8th-grade boys—Aviation Show (models for sale)
9th-grade boys—The Igloo (ice cream)
9th-grade girls—Cosmopolitan Theater (movies)
Girls teacher-training class—The French Shoppe (pastries)

The older grades were to be general assistants where needed. This, and other ventures for the offering, were prayed about and so made worshipful. The ninth-grade boys made a map showing the splendid record of the Christian missionaries in each country. Others wrote essays on offerings. One of the prayer leaflets they compiled was used in a Montana ranch isolated from the Church. (See page 67 for "Questions and Assignments Used in Compiling the Lenten Prayer Leaflet.")

The talks given at the Church School Sunday services were assigned by each class to definite pupils. Those chosen were provided with the national literature and any extra information needed. As a different field was used each Sunday, the news items collected by the mothers were an effective help.

Each pupil speaker was requested to come to the parish office to discuss his or her talk two weeks before the date on which it was to be presented. As with the other leaders, they were also asked to come on the day before to try out voices and to learn where to stand, etc., also to pray for the message to help others. One fourth-grader had to talk on China. Most of her talk was about food and clothes. When asked why she had chosen these in preference to other subjects which seemed of more interest to the questioner, she replied that those were the things she was interested in and so others would be too. Again, a child saw clearly how to gain the interest of other boys and girls.

Some of these Lenten speakers chose to wear national costumes. Others just spoke simply as Americans telling a story. We found that fourth-graders could do more than we expected in speaking and in choosing and compiling prayers. The teachers co-operated effectively because there was no feeling that these things were taking valuable time from a set course. These were courses and units of study and led to a deeper interest in the prescribed courses when they were attempted again. They enriched worship interest and reality. All study was basd on worship and all the activities connected with it, because God was our partner in all parts of our living, not only in the Church work.

3. A DAY OF PRAYER

Although this came, for these boys and girls, as a climax for their Lenten study and plans, it might be a preparation for Lent in the plans of another council if they so chose. For that reason this worship experience is being described first.

The reason it came as a climax was a natural one. The women had had a Day of Prayer as the climax of their Lenten study. This was a new idea to the boys and girls when they heard of it through announcements and in their homes. They asked, "Why can't we have one too?"

They were told by the Rector that he approved very highly provided they would organize and conduct it themselves. They could ask for any counselling they needed but it must be *their* day. They were delighted and asked how it was done. Then they decided to prepare their own outlines, using others as guides. They planned to go into church by two's in case anyone might be fearful of being in the church building alone. This proved wise for some of the younger ones. The two pupils could either each take half of the allotted fifteen minutes, or they could kneel and pray together at the litany desk in the center aisle. If they knelt there separately, the other one was instructed to kneel or sit quietly in one of the front pews while waiting.

The outlines were prepared by an older class. The Advent outline of intercessions for the parish and diocese was used as a guide. The theme was world missions and peace as an outcome of the Lenten study of missions and world needs. When finished and approved, the outlines were mimeographed for Church use. They consisted of statements of fact and then prayers for the needs stated. They began with a brief statement about prayer. It was very simple, with few words, and rightly so. Being alone in the church was a new experience for many, and they needed time to meditate on this in addition to words for intercession.

Each class was asked for volunteers. No one was required to co-operate. A list of those volunteering and a schedule of times assigned were made. They were asked to wait in the parish office when they came. Those in church were asked to report to the office before leaving so that the two pupils waiting would know when to enter. This gave the director an opportunity to note any fear or nervousness, also to hear the expressions which resulted. One girl joyfully reported that she had looked at the watch tied on the litany desk and said a prayer every minute. She had missed the point of meditation but had given what she thought was complete devotion. Perhaps it was. They all took it very seriously. They felt adult about doing it, you could see.

Among the group of volunteers were two older boys who had been a trial to most of their teachers. They had shown little interest in worship before. They wanted to come together. The director, fearing mischief was planned, went very quietly into the rear of the church. She came out much ashamed. No boys could have been more reverent. They never even whispered to each other. We had previously failed to meet their spiritual needs with a challenge which to them seemed vital. From then on they were two of the most helpful boys in the school. One boy who was later chosen as a summer conference delegate was much surprised. He came to the office the day after he was chosen and asked,

"Why did you choose me?" He was told that we realized he had ability for leadership because he had shown it in the wrong way. We wanted to give him an opportunity to see whether he might like to use it in good ways to help other boys and girls. That was the turning point in his spiritual life. He did use it very earnestly for the good of all the young people. He became a leader in all the youth activities of the Church.

Only two small couples asked the director to go into the church while they were there. By questioning, the fear was discovered to be of "bad people" who might be in there, and not fear of God. It was the result of over-fearful parents. The director's presence released their youthful thoughts for worship of the God they did not fear physically.

4. SUGGESTIONS FOR ORGANIZING A DAY OF PRAYER

1. Explain what a Day of Prayer is—that it is a day when those who care enough to do so, come together, or come one or two at a time, during most of the hours of the day, to pray for a special need or needs.

2. If it has not already been done, it would be most valuable to discuss what prayer is and the different kinds of prayer e.g.—adoration, meditation, intercession, thanksgiving, etc. This might be used to make the day most helpful to both the intercessor and to the people for whom they plan to pray.

3. Appoint a committee on arrangements to plan with the Rector for the day, the preparation of the Church School and congregation, and the physical appointments necessary.

4. Appoint the necessary sub-committees (a) to see that the prayer books, hymnals and Bibles are in place and copies of the program available for all who may come in, in addition to the intercessors; (b) to see that a time-piece is tied to the special prayer desk (a watch) for those not having one; (c) to compile the list of those willing to act as intercessors and have typed lists available in the church and in the parish office (this should note the times promised by each); (d) to notify the adult groups and to ask for their prayers; (e) to explain the arrangements to the Church School pupils and ask their prayers. (This gives those unable to come a share in the day. Copies of the program might be sent to the homes, also.)

5. The day should be planned far enough ahead to allow for an intelligent and prayerful preparation of the program by the pupils.

6. Ask the Rector to announce the Day of Prayer to the whole congregation at least three Sundays before the date on which it is to be held, requesting their prayers and cooperation as friends and parents of the pupils.

7. Request each intercessor to come to the church at least a few minutes before his or her period of intercession, to avoid making others wait, also to avoid any interim between intercessors. Each intercessor should be asked to report first to the parish office or to a teacher or officer in charge. If there seems to be any timidity about being alone in the church building, someone should be available to go in to pray with that pupil.

8. Suggest in the preparation that the intercessors avoid any unnecessary talking or greetings in the church. This will avoid any interruptions for the worship of others.

9. Request any who have to cancel their time to notify the person in charge. Suggest that they use the program of intercessions at home either alone or with their family.
10. Plan to have some kind of evaluation discussion with the pupils afterwards, also with the teachers and parents.

5. A DAILY PRAYER LEAFLET FOR USE DURING LENT*

SUNDAY

Today, let us think of those in trouble or need of any kind, particularly those who are being hurt by unemployment.

Christ has help and sympathy for all people. To help us to pray for them, let us read St. Luke 11:2-10; St. John 14; 16:32-33; 6:35.

PRAYER FOR THOSE IN NEED

O God, with whom nothing is impossible, grant us courage and strength from communion with Thee, so that we may meet all hardships bravely, and never fail to think brave thoughts, to speak brave words, and to do brave deeds. We ask this in Jesus Christ's Name. *Amen.*

A QUESTION TO ASK YOURSELF

Am I doing as much as I can for those who are in trouble, or need?

"Thy Kingdom Come"

MONDAY

Today, let us think of those who are lonely, over-tired, or afraid, especially those who do not know that Christ is their Friend to whom they can go through prayer.

* This Prayer Leaflet was prepared by a ninth grade class of girls. See page 54 for comments on compiling the leaflet.

Christ knew how to get strength and comfort from our heavenly Father. Let us read how He did it in St. Luke 23; St. Matthew 11:28-30, to help us to pray.

PRAYER FOR THE DISCOURAGED

O God, who art ever ready to help us all in our problems, we beseech Thee to guide those who struggle blindly here and in far lands. May the comfort which Christ supplies meet all their needs and open their lives to Him. We ask it for Jesus' sake. *Amen.*

A QUESTION TO ASK YOURSELF

Do I try to comfort those who are afraid?

"Thy Kingdom Come"

TUESDAY

Today, let us pray for all who are ill, whether near or far away, remembering our war veterans who suffered hurt for us.

Christ knew how to help people who were ill and suffering. Let us read about it in St. Luke 4:38-41; St. Mark 1:40-42; St. Matthew 15:30.

PRAYER FOR THOSE WHO ARE ILL

O loving Father, help those who are ill and suffering to increase their trust in Thee through a more prayerful study of Christ's life and teachings. Give them a sure faith and real fellowship with Thee through faithful prayer and communion. Fill their hearts and minds with that "peace which passeth human understanding," and lead us all to try earnestly to grow more like Jesus. In His Name we ask it. *Amen.*

A QUESTION TO ASK YOURSELF

Do I remember to pray for all who are ill and suffering?

"Thy Kingdom Come"

WEDNESDAY

Today, let us pray for those who are bearing big responsibilities for the Church's work; our missionaries, bishops and Rector.

Christ has the biggest responsibility of all. To help us to do our part, let us read about Him in St. Luke 4:14-18; St. John 14:15-21; St. Matthew 21:22.

PRAYER FOR THOSE WHO BEAR RESPONSIBILITIES

Grant, O Lord, to all those who carry heavy responsibilities for spreading Thy kingdom in this world, the strength to work in Thy way for everyone whom they are trying to help. Grant them understanding of the feelings and needs of others, deepen the power of Christ in their hearts and minds, so that through their lives the lives they seek to win may be drawn closer to Thee. Grant them courage for their many hardships and problems in these trying days; and open our hearts to the need of loyally working with them in carrying on Thy work for Thy sake. *Amen.*

A QUESTION TO ASK YOURSELF

Am I doing my part to help those who bear big responsibilities for our Church?

"Thy Kingdom Come"

THURSDAY

Today, let us think of those who are causing wars and anguish for others because they lack an understanding of God's love, praying that they may find and know Christ's way of life.

Christ wanted people to be kind to each other and to forgive those who hurt them. Let us read St. Luke 23:33-34; St. Mark 11:25; St. Matthew 5:44-48; 28:16-20.

Prayer for Workers Against the Kingdom

O Saviour of the world, give us a sincere loathing for evil ways and inspire us with life's highest ideals. Grant, to those who are seeking an understanding of Thy love, the power, through their example and work, to change the thoughts of those now causing wars and strife, turning wrong efforts to the cause of Thy Kingdom in this world, to Thy honor and glory. *Amen.*

A Question to Ask Yourself

Do I try to remember that my example will help or hurt someone else each day?

"Thy Kingdom Come"

FRIDAY

Today, let us pray that the pupils, teachers, and officers of our Church School and the members of our parish may work faithfully and sincerely to learn to know Christ through worship and study together, so that others will be drawn to Him by what we say and do.

Let us read what Christ said about how we may be a part of His Kingdom in St. Luke 17:21; St. John 15:4, 5, 7, 10; 14:12-14.

Prayer for Our Church School and Parish

Our Father, we pray Thee to increase our loyalty and fellowship with Christ. May we keep Him always in our thoughts as our pattern day by day. May we seek to draw closer to Him through our worship and study, this Lenten season, so that we may have the strength and power to serve His Kingdom in all we do and say, through Jesus Christ our Lord. *Amen.*

A Question to Ask Yourself

Am I doing my full part to try to know Christ better through worship and study?

"Thy Kingdom Come"

SATURDAY

Today, let us pray that each of us may be so enthusiastic about all that we can do to make Christ's Kingdom come that we will give unselfishly of our time, money and prayers to help, not only our own country, but all the world.

Read what Christ wanted us to do about His Kingdom in St. Luke 22:29, 32; St. Matthew 28: 16-20; St. Mark 12:30-31.

Prayer for Personal Loyalty

O loving Father, help me to love Thee with my whole self. Through my study of our Lord's life and teachings and of the world's need of His Kingdom, may I be inspired to serve Thee not only with my lips but in my daily living, for the sake of our Lord who gave His life for us. *Amen.*

A Question to Ask Yourself

Am I as willing and cheerful as I might be in giving my time, money, and thoughts to the carrying on of Christ's work?

"Thy Kingdom Come"

6. QUESTIONS AND ASSIGNMENTS USED IN COMPILING THE LENTEN PRAYER LEAFLET

I. Are Bible readings a help in preparing for prayer? Why? Is it helpful to just think of God, or to hold in our minds a mental picture of how our Lord might have looked, before we begin to pray?

What Bible readings could we use to help people to understand that Christ wanted us to be missionaries?

What mental picture of Christ would help us in thinking

of needs in foreign countries—medical help, teaching, etc.?

How does it help us to take time for prayer even though we know that Christ wants our best happiness and we can trust Him?

ASSIGNMENT A (committee)

Bring in a list of seven Bible passages which would help if used for people having the following needs:

1. People who are ill.
2. People who are afraid.
3. People who are enduring persecution.
4. Missionaries who are lonely and weary.
5. People who are unemployed and in need.
6. People who have heavy responsibilities for the Church's work.
7. People who are fighting Christianity through ignorance of it.

II. What needs of the Church School would you include in a prayer to make it of more use in bringing in Christ's Kingdom on earth?

ASSIGNMENT B (committee)

Bring in a list of the needs of the Church School and formulate a prayer we might use in our leaflet for Lent.

III. What things prevent us, personally, from living up to the things Christ wants us to do for His kingdom and to bring spiritual growth in our own lives?

1. Do we choose to give time for prayer or do we allow other things to interfere?
2. Do we allow things to make us irritable with others?

3. Do we give enough thought to the plans of others when they interfere with our own?
4. Do we think of this life as a school for eternal life in a way that helps us to realize which are the important matters or do we allow material things to have first place when there is a choice?
5. What things are lasting things?

ASSIGNMENT C (committee)

Bring in a list of questions (perhaps seven—one for each day) which would help the pupils to think about strengthening their spiritual life. This is called self-examination and is a form of prayer. There is the danger of using it sometimes to make yourself feel self-righteous by asking only the questions you can answer without any feeling of failure. It is the other questions we should use.

IV. How would you list the daily subjects if you had to make out a reading and prayer outline for each day of the week, using one for the parish, one for the diocesan and national Church work, and others for mission fields? Would you group the needs or would you have the same needs, if they were there, listed under each field?

ASSIGNMENT D (committee)

Write out an outline for each of the above methods which could be used for a folder of four pages:
1. Day.
2. Subject.
3. Bible reading or meditation.
4. Statement of needs.
5. Personal question of self-examination.
6. Prayer.

V. EASTER AND WHITSUNDAY PLANS

1. THE EASTER SERVICE AND PAGEANT

The Easter service had to fulfill two challenges—the presentation of the offering in a way that told of its need and gave it value as an act of worship to the givers, and the telling of the Easter story to the congregation.

The council could find nothing that quite pleased them. A spoken pageant or play was out of the question. It was the time of year when church windows might have to be open. The year before the young people had given a beautiful spoken play. The dress rehearsal had been fine. But on Sunday the outside traffic had drowned out every voice and disappointed everyone. The council decided to create its own pageant. Ideas were acceptable from young and old. One man teacher, an electrician, offered to electrify the cross usually used to receive the piled-in small offering boxes. It was about five feet high. He made it glow gradually in the center as the boxes filled it. This was very effective.

The Bible story was chosen as the main theme. The Rector's voice was always clearly heard, so they asked him to be the reader of the story from the pulpit. The action was to take place in the chancel with the choir in their usual places. The sanctuary, where the altar stood, was to be cut off from view by using wall-board screens covered with a gray painted cloth to represent the Easter tomb. The inside of the tomb was meant to glow gradually, like the cross, on Easter morning. They lined it with gold paper, only to find that it reflected black, but that was changed in time, and the result was very effective with the glory it represented.

The main outline of the pageant or pantomime was the coming of boys and girls, friends of Jesus, to the tomb. These children were in Eastern costumes. They were frightened, disappointed, and resentful when they found two Roman soldiers guarding the tomb which was closed by a huge circle representing the stone. The soldiers tried to make friends, but the children ran away. One boy shrugged off the soldier's hand and flung himself down before the tomb so realistically that some people in the congregation thought he had fainted. The story continued with Mary Magdalene coming with flowers and spice. She lifted and comforted the boy and led him off.

Organ music rumbling represented the breaking open of the tomb (the stone was pulled aside by ropes from the side). Then Easter music and the gradually glowing light symbolized the rising of Christ. The three Marys appeared and acted out their amazement. After hearing the reader read the angel's message, they hurried off. Mary Magdalene came as the reader told the story of the appearance of our Lord. She hurried off after the reading and Peter and John appeared and acted out that part of the Easter story. Then Mary Magdalene appeared leading the children, the boy she had comforted running ahead. They drew her towards the cross and grouped around it as the reader bade the pupils bring their offerings to the cross. The cross began to glow as the offering boxes were placed in it. When all were piled round or in the cross, and when the pupils were back in their seats, a missionary hymn was sung. During the singing of this hymn five boys and girls, symbolizing the five races in color and costume, came slowly and as if fearfully and yet hopefully down the center aisle and saw the cross gladly. They ran to it and knelt before it, making a tableau of the two sets of children and of Mary Magdalene. During the blessing, all knelt. During the final hymn the Palestinian children and Mary Magdalene withdrew through the entrance near the altar rail, symbolizing their living as of another world. The five children of different races withdrew down the center aisle, symbolizing their going back to tell others. The choir followed and the service was over, the lights in the tomb and cross continuing to glow until the congregation had left.

This simple pageant could be copied by any church and, like the Christmas one, there is little tension in it for anyone preparing it.

It was compiled, acted, and criticized by the pupils themselves. Using those who were not acting at the time as critics was a very real experience for them, also a new one. When Peter swiftly ran to the tomb, they made him hear the story of what had happened to Peter to make him one of the weariest and saddest of the apostles. Peter repeated his entrance in a weary, hopeless manner and let John run ahead. Being in it, they all had an interest in having each act be the best.

They decided that the children our Lord knew would surely have stolen away to get to his tomb with flowers (the modern gift). They also decided that Mary Magdalene, being kind, would have gone to tell them and have brought them to see the glowing tomb for themselves, after telling her story of seeing Jesus Christ as the risen Lord and knowing surely that it was true.

No actor had any words to speak. The story was told entirely by the reader, by the music, by the hymns, and by their actions. Each character was challenged with the story if he or she did not portray the actions well. They had to feel the story as reality.

2. WHITSUNDAY—A BIRTHDAY THANK OFFERING SERVICE

Whitsunday, being celebrated as the birthday of the Church, was traditionally chosen by the national Church office as the day when the Church Schools should give a birthday thank offering for some mission need. It was another opportunity for the student council to function.

Since it was a well-known activity, like the Lenten offering, plans were begun early in the school year. Mimeographed letters were mailed out, with a birthday prayer card and a printed leaflet in each about the place to which the offering was nationally designated. The special objective of the letter was to tell why we should be thankful for birthdays. It also announced the showing of slides on the mission field and invited the parents for the next Sunday session to see the slides. The *Council Courier* also carried an item which told about the chapel which the offering was to build at a mission school, and announced, "The Birthday Thank Offering is also a way of sharing our birthday happiness not only with our families and friends but with other boys and girls farther away. Through it we enlarge the circle of our friendship until it becomes worldwide."

The service was planned by one of the classes around the theme of missions and thanksgiving. One of the fathers, also a teacher, prepared with the help of his pupils a model of the church which was to be built with the offerings. It was very intriguing. It rang a bell for every offering dropped through its spire. It lit up all its stained-glass windows (painted parchment Christmas-card cut-outs) to show that light and joy were being given with the Gospel. Every boy and girl looked forward to giving his or her offering. If the model had not been explained symbolically it might have been a distraction to worship. It was fun too. Our little model church went to diocesan meetings. We were very proud of it. The grown-ups were intrigued by it too. They planned a birthday party for the whole parish in which the adults entertained the pupils, dividing to different floors afterwards, for games. No admission was charged, but Birth-day Offerings were requested, and the grown-ups had fun lighting up the little church and ringing the bell. This party gave an opportunity to call on talent in the parish. We knew of this talent because it had been included in the every-member canvass.

One singer in a long lettuce-green dress—a person who hardly ever came to Church and whom we were anxious to interest—almost had her Church career ended by the magician's rabbit. The rabbit escaped to nibble at the lettuce, but was rescued in time, just as it started to disappear under the long dress. The magician was also a Church member giving hobby talent.

All this was *before* the Whitsunday service. That was the climax of the year's giving when the complete offering was presented at the altar and a blessing asked upon its use for others.

VI. THE CHURCH SCHOOL COMMUNION SERVICE

1. PLANNING THE SERVICE

This is a service which of necessity needs a superimposed form. Our Lord gave us the original form and each part of the Church has developed its own ritual and ceremonial around that form. Even in the same Church group, there will be differences in the drama of its presentation. However, it is attractive to children because of this drama, even before they know anything about the meaning of the service. As the knowledge of its meaning grows, the service, too, should grow richer for them. We know, however, that in many cases the irreverence of junior boys and girls shows that the form has lasted but the meaning and richness for them has somehow been lost, at least temporarily.

Again, we decided to ask the boys and girls why. The answer was quick and unanimous—"We don't know what it means"—"It's so long"—"We get uncomfortable"—"We don't know what a lot of the words mean." These were usually the answers from those not receiving communion. Some of the older ones thought, "It is hard to keep your thoughts going with the words for so long and you begin thinking of other things before you know it"; also, "People keep going out and disturbing the others."

They were told that in some churches a form of explanation is given by a reader in between the parts of the service, the celebrant or priest just reading the service. They liked the idea, and asked if they could try it too. This was one service where they were willing to have the Rector do the compiling. This seemed necessary to them and to the Rector as well. Such a form was compiled to fit our form of service. Other forms have been used to fit other forms and teachings, according to the type of churchmanship. Each celebrant should approve his own for the sake of sincerity and to avoid confusion of teaching in his church. As we wanted ours to explain some of the meaning even for the youngest junior-age fourth-grader, it needed to be in the simplest form. It may seem too simple and some parts may seem unnecessary. Each person needs to decide for his own group. An outline of the instructions used is given on page 77.

We did discover some other things about our service which hindered or helped the worship. Inviting the parents for our first instruction service almost caused a feud. Some had the bad habit of making a disturbing exodus in the middle of the service when they were not going to receive communion. The pupils were very disturbed when this happened at their service. They had studied the instructions and realized that we owe a courtesy to our Lord even more than to other hosts or hostesses when we accept an invitation to a supper. It was the Lord's Supper. They sensed an obligation to Him.

They took the problem to the Rector and to the parents at the parents' meeting, much to the parents' chagrin and edification. It never happened again. The parents felt the need of an instructional service, too, and came the next time with a different attitude—and stayed.

In using the service we discovered some physical aids of value also. At the first service the reader knelt at the litany desk in the front of the center aisle. The pupils in the rear could not hear very well as his voice was thrown forward.

The priest read only the service, pausing for the instruction sentences to be read (his copy was his guide). At the second service the reader sat and knelt in the choir stalls. A teacher noticed that many of the pupils looked up each time the reader spoke. It was disturbing their worship. The final and best decision made was to have the reader kneel at the litany desk which was placed at the rear in the center aisle, behind the worshippers. Some looked back during the first instruction but not afterwards. The reader became just a voice, as we had hoped. Even the younger children seemed more interested and all showed a growing reverence during the service. It had become *their* service, specially planned to meet their needs instead of just meeting the needs of adults. The pauses relieved the feeling of length which one voice had evidently given, and it made that one voice more important as it came to them from the altar. The contrast seemed to help. Pupils began to ask questions in their classes. The teachers found the service more full of worship for themselves, too, as the tensions of restless children were relieved. Strangely, although the service was longer, the tensions were less noticeable. The verdict was that they "liked it now." It could not relieve the necessity for physical moving which small growing bodies need, but it did relieve the irreverent inattention of the junior-age pupils.

2. INSTRUCTIONS FOR A CHURCH SCHOOL COMMUNION SERVICE

(The letter "I" is used for the Instructor and "P" for the Priest. Service is from the Episcopal Book of Common Prayer.)

I.—The processional hymn is number ooo.

The Priest enters after the hymn is finished and the choir is in place. (Here an instruction on the preparation of the altar may be given.)

P.—Let us pray. (*While the Priest makes his personal preparation the pupils may be instructed on their personal preparation for this service and prepared for the Collect for Purity.*)

I.—Turn to page 67 of your Prayer Book. (*Pause*)

In the first fine print under the title it says: "And the Priest, standing reverently before the Holy Table, shall say The Lord's Prayer and the Collect following." So our Priest and Rector stands now before the Holy Table, or Altar, ready, as our elder person or Priest, to present our offerings to God and to bring God's gift to us. While he is saying the Lord's Prayer, as his prayer of preparation, let us *kneel* and pray silently for him and for ourselves that we may each take a full and loving part in the service, whether we are confirmed and ready to receive the sacrament personally or not.

P.—The Lord's Prayer.

The Collect for Purity.

I.—While the Priest reads the laws which God has given to us to keep, we are going to think about our own thoughts and actions, and in response we are going to ask God's forgiveness for any wrong things we have done and ask for His help and power to enable us to obey Him in the future.

P.—The Commandments or Summary of the Law.

The responses or Kyrie. (Choir and congregation)

The Collect and Versicles.

I.—Now, keeping your place on page 70, turn to page —

to the prayer which is called the Collect for ————.
After the prayer we will listen to the teaching of the
Epistle following it. (*Explain what an Epistle is, if
necessary.*)

P.—*The Collect for the Day.*
   The Epistle.

I.—Now we *stand* to hear the words of Christ from the
writings of one of His first apostles. (*Pause*)

After the Gospel is announced it will be read, but
before it is read we acknowledge His greatness in our
lives by saying together "Glory be to Thee, O Lord."
At the close of the reading we give Christ praise for His
gift.

P.—*The Gospel.*

I.—We remain standing now and pledge our allegiance to
God by all saying together the Nicene Creed on page 71.

P.—*The Nicene Creed.*
   (*Notices and address here if desired.*)

I.—As good stewards of the material gifts which God has
given to us, we now offer our money gifts to Him for
His work so that we may share in it as His partners.

P.—*The Offertory Sentence.*
   The Anthem.
   Presentation of the Offerings and the Doxology.

I.—Turn to page 74. (*Pause*)

Having now made to God our offerings of our obedience to His law, our faith through the Creed, and our
gifts for His work, we are now going to offer our
prayers for others. We *kneel* for prayer.

P.—*The Prayer for the Whole State of Christ's Church.*

I.—Through our responses to God's law, we confessed our
particular personal faults. The Priest now calls upon us

to repent and to confess those faults which we all commit, after which we confess them by all saying together the General Confession. Then the Priest, speaking as God's appointed officer, announces God's forgiveness to those who are truly sorry. After that the Priest says the comfortable or strengthening words said by or concerning Christ.

P.—*The General Confession.*
The Absolution.
The Comfortable Words.

I.—Our Lord said, "Joy shall be in heaven over one sinner that repenteth." So, we join with the angels in heaven, and with all God's people who have left this earth and are with Christ in Paradise, in praising God for His goodness. The Priest invites us to lift up our hearts in thanksgiving.

P.—*The Sursum Corda.*
The Sanctus.

I.—Turn to page 80. (*Pause*)

The long prayer on this page and the next is called the prayer of consecration or the setting apart for holy use. It is divided into four parts. In the first part the Priest repeats the words and acts of our Lord at the Last Supper. In the second part we offer the bread and the wine to God the Father to use for His purpose. In the third part we ask God to sanctify the bread and the wine—that is, to use them for the holy purpose of bringing to us the values which our Lord wanted us to have when He gave his life—His Body and His Blood—for us. In the fourth part we humbly offer ourselves, our souls and bodies, for the holy use of carrying those values and gifts to other people in God's world.

This prayer is followed by our Lord's own prayer, on page 82.

P.—*The Prayer of Consecration.*
The Lord's Prayer.

I.—Now the Priest, speaking as the representative of all who are to come to the Lord's Table, begs God's help that all who come may understand how high and holy is their privilege, and may afterwards feel that our Lord is truly living in their hearts and lives.

P.—*The Prayer of Humble Access.*

I.—The priest and the choir first receive the bread and the wine. Afterwards the Priest stands and turns to the congregation with the paten, or Bread plate, in his hands. At that time, those who have been confirmed may *go forward* and kneel at the sanctuary rail until they have received both the Bread and the Wine. The others will remain quietly on their knees, praying silently for those who go to receive their Communion, for themselves, for their loved ones, and for all God's loved ones everywhere.

I.—(*After all have received*) Let us all remain *kneeling* now while the Priest says for us our thanksgiving to God for all His goodness to us, and for showing us ways in which we may serve Him loyally and gratefully as members of His Church.

P.—*The Prayer of Thanksgiving.*

I.—Now we will all *stand* for the hymn of praise called the *Gloria in Excelsis*. We turn to page — and say (or sing) this with the Priest.

P.—*The Gloria in Excelsis.*

I.—Now we kneel again to receive the benediction or blessing to help us to take God's peace and love out to our homes, our community, and wherever we go.

P.—*The Benediction.*

I.—After the recessional hymn we will *kneel* again to thank God for allowing us to share in this holy service and, as a sign of respect and gratitude for this privilege, we will *remain kneeling* until the altar candles, the symbols of the Presence of our Lord, have been put out. Then we will quietly leave the church.

The recessional hymn is number —.

VII. A COMMENCEMENT SERVICE AND SUMMER WORSHIP PLANS

1. A COMMENCEMENT SERVICE

This service was the climax of our year's work and worship, and the Rector decided that the boys and girls had earned the reward of publicity, and so it was held at the time of the main congregational service. In that way it would also be educational for the parish members who had little contact with the school.

As previously noted, honor tests had been given, and this was the service when certificates for these tests, and for class effort and attendance would be awarded to the boys and girls who had earned them. There was an adult class, but this was not included in the awards. The choir awards were made at this service too. The names of those chosen to attend summer conferences at the expense of the Church were also announced.

The council decided that there should be talks by four of the pupils to tell what they felt the Church School had done in worship, study, service, and fellowship. One of the speakers chosen was from the fourth grade, one from the sixth, one from the eighth, and one from the tenth. The Rector was asked to give a brief address also. These talks were limited to five minutes and took the place of the sermon. They were sermons of a very real kind to those who listened.

To avoid the addresses being a list of things done rather

than a summing up of the real values, the council had edited and printed in the *Council Courier* June issue a complete service report under these four headings. In this the money gifts were also listed and itemized, a total of almost eight hundred dollars, in addition to all the material gifts. These money and material gifts were also itemized by place —parish, diocese, nation, and world. It must have amazed many parents.

2. HOME AND SUMMER WORSHIP

During the year there had been constant emphasis on taking worship into the home. This the council had done by letters, worship leaflets, the *Council Courier*, and printed national leaflets which were sometimes enclosed with other items in mailing. There had also been a growing use of home "Prayer Corners" where a small shelf or table was set aside as a home altar to remind the boys and girls of worship. One of the items in the Service Report was "Hung religious pictures for others to see"; another was "Sent lessons and letters to invalid children." Other items concerned service to the aged and to the adult invalids of the Church. The emphasis was that the reason for everything was, "Go ye into all the world and preach the Gospel to every creature." You sensed it in every council meeting once they caught the joy of it. The school had outgoing joy instead of ingrowing pains.

When summer approached there was a mixed feeling of release from the ever-growing demands which such a program made on the leaders, satisfaction from a job well done, regret that the fellowship was not to be as often, and anticipation of the next year. The things said showed all this. The pupils needed to feel that the Church was not just a seasonal effort, but that they needed a change of effort for relaxation. They were told of a plan, used at another parish, where a summer folder for home services was given out in June—a folder which could be used anywhere by anyone or any family. They wanted to see it and were shown a copy.

Since they enjoyed creating things of their own by now, they wanted to have their own program on a different theme. After much discussion, the theme of the needs of employers and employees was chosen. This may seem a strange theme for children, but it was a time of unemployment and worry in many of the homes. As usual, they had chosen the best theme for their homes.

The main thought was the need of employers and employees to understand and use Christ's teachings. They had adult help with the outline to find the places in the Gospel where these teachings were given, but most of the planning was their own, after they had had the meaning of the teachings explained. It was not an easy theme, they found, and it should have been started earlier for them to gain the most benefit from the study. But that was our fault and not theirs. Such a folder should have been a unit of study for at least half the year. However, the homes, using it, were having a summer unit of study together. Perhaps exploring it together had more value to the whole family.

To give additional value to this activity the boys and girls were given suggestions about using it outdoors, on the beach, in a field, setting up an outdoor cross for a family chapel, etc. They were also helped to feel that the leadership they had given in the Church School worship might take more courage to suggest at home, but that a good way to begin was to try. If they could not create a family opportunity, it was suggested that they might gather together a group of playmates for a service where taking turns in leading would be fun. This method was most frequently reported in the fall, but no report was required, and so we have no record as to how many parents lacked the courage and lost the opportunity for a closer Christian relationship. Many used it.

3. LETTER AND SUMMER HOME WORSHIP FOLDER

The Letter

DEAR MEMBERS OF THE CHURCH SCHOOL:

A good word to think about during your summer holidays is recreation. People sometimes think of it as meaning re-creation of body and mind. It should also mean re-creating the spirit. The spirit is the real driving power of life, while the body and mind are just instruments through which the spirit expresses itself. For that reason we are asking you, as a disciple of our Lord, to spare a few minutes each day during your vacation to try to find out what He teaches as the truly happy way of living.

Here are some suggestions to help you to re-create your spirit:

1. Beginning on Sunday, use daily each week the enclosed folder called "Stories Our Lord Told Us." These stories are called parables. A parable is a story with a hidden meaning. Some stories are told just for fun, but our Lord's stories were told to help us to understand the rules of unselfish living. The meaning was hidden so that we might each think it

out for our own lives. God respects us too much to do all our thinking for us. We must decide for ourselves as our Lord did. He helped us to make good decisions by proving in His own life that the unselfish life is the only truly happy one. We help other people in the same way when we make good decisions.

2. Either with your family, or by yourself, read the Bible reading and use the prayer suggested in the folder. To help you to remember to be faithful in giving part of each day to God, mark each day with a circle if you have used the suggested reading and prayer. We should like to see your record in October, if you care to show it to us, but we will return the folder to you to keep.

3. Try to find the hidden meanings in the stories. Talk over with your family and your friends how people today can use those meanings in their daily living. The world needs guidance. This study will help you to become a leader in helping others to find understanding also.

4. If you like to write, make up stories of your own on our Lord's way of living as shown in these parables. They could be stories of today. Bring these stories back with you and we will choose the best ones to tell at our Church School services. This may help those who have not tried to find the meanings.

5. If you are spending your vacation where there are no Church services which you can attend, have an outdoor or indoor service of your own. Invite your friends and family to help you. Use the hymns suggested, or choose your own hymns and prayers, and share the service.

6. Help the Church to provide places to teach our Lord's way of living to others by continuing your weekly offering during your vacation. Bring the offering with you in the

fall to be credited to the offering of the school for the Parish House Fund, the fund the Student Council chose for this offering.

We hope you will all be present to help to welcome each other in the fall to a new year of school companionship. Some will be asked to make up neglected work during the summer. We are sure you will want to do this so that you may go on with your classmates to new work. We are giving you this opportunity because we want to help you to know how to serve and follow our Lord and to be worthwhile workers in His Church, as you promised at your Baptism. It is for you to decide whether you keep your promise and follow Him. No one can do it for you. We can only help you by showing you the way which our Lord gave to all of us to try.

Before you go away, try to take time to look through your books and magazines. Bring to the Parish House any which you would like to share with other boys and girls who have very few. Mark the package "Church Periodical Club" and leave it in the office. This is one way in which we can share our good times with others this summer.

Faithfully yours,
THE CHURCH SCHOOL STAFF

The Folder

STORIES OUR LORD TOLD US

An Invitation to a Party
June — (4th Sunday after Trinity)   1 2 3 4 5 6 7
St. Luke 14:12-24. What do you think would happen to the world if we all made excuses that we were too busy to take

time for God? Could we live without God's gifts? What excuses do you make?

PRAYER: "For Joy in God's Creation" (Family Prayer Section)

HYMNS: "All things bright and beautiful—"
"Hushed was the evening hymn—"
"O Lord of heaven and earth and sea—"

SOME SEEDS THAT GOT LOST

June — (5th Sunday after Trinity)   1 2 3 4 5 6 7
St. Mark 4:1-20. What are some of the things which keep people from growing into our Lord's way of living?

PRAYER: The Collect for "The Transfiguration of Christ"

HYMNS: "Saviour, teach me, day by day—"
"O Jesus, Thou art standing—"
"Come labor on. Who dares stand idle—"

AN EMPLOYER WHO PLAYED FAIR AND SOME WORKERS WHO WERE GREEDY

July — (6th Sunday after Trinity)   1 2 3 4 5 6 7
St. Matthew 20:1-16. How should our nation treat those who are unemployed through no fault of their own, while they wait to be hired?

PRAYER: "For Social Justice" (Prayers and Thanksgiving section)

HYMNS: "There is a green hill far away—"
"Lord God of Hosts, Whose mighty hand—"
"God of our fathers, Whose almighty hand—"

TWO BUILDERS

July — (7th Sunday after Trinity)   1 2 3 4 5 6 7
St. Luke 6:45-49. Whose teachings are like the rock? In building our lives, what is like the sand?

PRAYER: Collect for "St. Simon and St. Jude"

HYMNS: "The Son of consolation, Moved by Thy law of
love—"

"We build our school on Thee, O Lord—"

"Jesus, with Thy Church abide—"

A RICH MAN WHO HOARDED

July — (8th Sunday after Trinity)   1 2 3 4 5 6 7

St. Luke 12:13-31. Why did the rich man seem wise to himself? Why was he really foolish?

PRAYER: "For faithfulness in the use of this world's goods"
(Family Prayer section)

HYMNS: "Faithful Shepherd, feed me—"

"Where cross the crowded ways of life—"

"Rise up, O men of God—"

A WORKER WHO WOULDN'T SHARE

July — (9th Sunday after Trinity)   1 2 3 4 5 6 7

St. Matthew 18:21-35. Which man in the story do you like
best? When we refuse to forgive and help people, which
man are we like?

PRAYER: "For Christian Service" (Prayers and Thanksgivings section)

HYMNS: "I think when I read—"

"Father in heaven, Who lovest all—"

"There's a wideness in God's mercy—"

THE WORKERS WHO CHEATED

July — (10th Sunday after Trinity)   1 2 3 4 5 6 7

St. Mark 12:1-12. Would you like to have these laborers
(husbandmen) working for you? Did they keep their
positions, or gain anything, in the end?

PRAYER: "For every man in his work" (Prayers and Thanksgivings section)

Hymns: "When Jesus left His Father's throne—"
He who would valiant be—"
"Dear Lord and Father of mankind—"

Two Brothers
August — (11th Sunday after Trinity)   1 2 3 4 5 6 7
St. Matthew 21:28-31. Which boy would you rather have for
your friend? Which one would you rather have on a football
team of which you were a member? Why?
Prayer: "For Children" (Prayers and Thanksgiving sec-
tion)
Hymns: "Breathe on me, Breath of God—"
"O Jesus, I have promised—"
"Master, no offering, costly and sweet—"

A Dangerous Journey
August — (12th Sunday after Trinity)   1 2 3 4 5 6 7
St. Luke 10:25-37. Was the Samaritan who helped in danger
of robbers too? Which men in the story felt most happy, do
you think—the Samaritan or the others? Why? Which was
the bravest man?
Prayer: Collect for "St. Andrew the Apostle"
Hymns: "Lord, speak to me—"
"Christ for the world we sing—"
"Once to every man and nation—"

A Lost Lamb
August — (13th Sunday after Trinity)   1 2 3 4 5 6 7
St. Luke 15:3-10. Can you think of any people who have
lost the Jesus' way of living? Should they be left alone to be
hurt, or should those who know the way try to help them to
find their way back?
Prayer: "For Prisoners" (Prayers and Thanksgivings section)

Hymns: "Saviour, like a shepherd lead us—"
"Lead us, O Father, in the paths of peace—"
"The King of love my Shepherd is—"

A Lost Boy

August — (14th Sunday after Trinity)   1 2 3 4 5 6 7
St. Luke 15:11-32. What made the father forgive and welcome the boy who ran away and forgot him? Could the father have helped the boy, no matter how much he wanted to, if the boy had not decided to trust his father and come back?

Prayer: Collect for "Ash Wednesday"

Hymns: "Children of the heavenly King—"
"Come gracious Spirit, heavenly Dove—"
"The morning light is breaking—"

A Man Who Was Ill

September — (15th Sunday after Trinity)   1 2 3 4 5 6 7
St. Luke 16:19-31. How can we help sick people? Do we hurt ourselves when we refuse kindness to those who are helpless?

Prayer: "For all poor, homeless or neglected folk" (Family Prayer section)

Hymns: "Blest be the tie that binds—"
"Father in heaven, Who lovest all—"
"At even, when the sun was set—"

A Man Who Pretended

September — (16th Sunday after Trinity)   1 2 3 4 5 6 7
St. Luke 18:9-14. Of what are we thinking when we pretend to pray just to seem good? What makes prayer real and helpful to ourselves and others?

Prayer: "For quiet confidence" (Family Prayer section)

HYMNS: "We love the place, O God—"
  "Fairest Lord Jesus—"
  "Our blest Redeemer, ere He breathed—"

THE COMING OF THE KING
September — (17th Sunday after Trinity)   1 2 3 4 5 6 7
St. Matthew 25:1-13. Did you ever miss a good time by not being ready? What was our Lord trying to tell His disciples by this story?
PRAYER: Collect for "The Twentieth Sunday after Trinity."
HYMNS: "Go, labour on! spend and be spent!—"
  "Hark! A thrilling voice is sounding—"
  "Hark! The voice eternal—"

(The prayer references are for the Episcopal BOOK OF COMMON PRAYER and the hymns from THE EPISCOPAL HYMNAL, copyright 1916.)

VIII. PRE-SCHOOL, KINDERGARTEN, AND PRIMARY WORSHIP

1. A PRE-SCHOOL SERVICE

Each year the Church held a special spring service and party for the babies and pre-school children and their mothers. This year the student council considered it part of their Church School work and asked to do the planning.

In discussing this service they realized that knowledge of their small brothers and sisters was helpful. It was decided that the service should have lots of music and be brief. They also decided that it should have prayers helpful to both the mothers and the children. They decided that the story or stories should be in the parish house, not in the church, because, otherwise, the babies would not understand and would be restless and spoil things for the older pre-school children.

Because taking care of babies was considered girls' work, the girls were assigned to the party session to help with simple games and with the refreshments. The boys preferred planning the service. Both helped with the choir.

There was not much creative work to be done with this activity, but the council learned several things—that the educational work and fellowship of the Church School begins when a child is born, or should—that little children have different worship needs, but worship may be very simple in realizing God as another loving member of the family circle

—that mothers of small children need God's help—that the example of older boys and girls is a responsibility in Christian life. It was an opportunity for the older pupils to realize their own importance as Christians to small children, instead of thinking of them as an irritating nuisance.

2. WORSHIP IN THE KINDERGARTEN

While all these worship activities were taking place in the older group under the guidance of the Student Council, the younger groups were not being neglected. They were less able to make their own plans and choices, but they were also more frankly uninterested where we made the wrong choices for them. They were at the questioning age. They, too, had a right to know in a simple way what it was all about.

Certain main things seemed necessary to co-ordinate their learning and worship. We soon realized that worship must be the basic theme if God was to be their real Companion. Stories, handwork, sand-tables, dramatics, became more interesting and vital to the teachers also when used in building towards worship. We also realized that little children have a simple clear directness in worship that adults often find it hard to achieve because of their lack of faith and trust. Using the theme of worship tied everything together—home, Church, day school, Church School, playmates, etc.

For those who had little or no home teaching about God before they came, it was necessary to build up their idea of a loving Creator and Companion through stories about the creation and what Jesus Christ told about His heavenly Father. The handwork and sand-table were a dramatization of these stories—not busy work. When we sang "Good Morning to You" we also said "Good morning" to God through a simple prayer. The children were given a typed prayer to take home to use every morning. Attitudes of prayer were explained as caretakers of our thoughts and those of others. The story of the giving of the Lord's Prayer was told and this was used as the main theme during the year.

Each week a picture was chosen and a clause explained simply through a talk or a story—a story if possible. Small replicas of the pictures were ordered and paper books were prepared for pasting by the mothers' afternoon group. As each clause was finished (sometimes it took more than one week), a picture was pasted in each child's book by him or her. Each one was told that, when finished, it could be taken home as a prayer book to use at home. The covers were each child's own creation in decoration when the books were finally completed. Some chose pictures of Jesus, some pictures of children, and some drew their own designs. The covers were revealing as the children were asked their reasons for their choice. The reasons also revealed to us some of our teaching faults.

In addition, when we came to "Thy Kingdom Come," they were asked if each would like to make an extra book for some boy or girl who had no church building and was taught by mail. This created an interest in the church building. We tried to help them to realize that the building was to help them to think of God and was not the only place where we could talk to Him.

One Sunday we visited the organ. A small boy was terrified. After leading him safely out we found that the vibrations and the noise had reminded him of thunder. We told the organist, and he showed the boy all the parts of the organ and where the sound came out, testing it by squeaks that grew louder. This ended the fear.

Instead of a circle, chairs began to be arranged "like Church." The children lit the candles on the small table altar in their room to "remind us of the happiness Jesus gave to everyone." They marched to hymn tunes and began to learn the meaning of some of the simpler hymns. These hymns were used by request in the special services the youngest children attended "to make them feel at home in God's House."

They dramatized for action—sometimes the story if it was simple enough, taking turns being different characters. For this the teacher closed her eyes, told them to move around on tip-toes, and then pointed and named a character. The one nearest where she pointed became the character. It was a fair way and avoided trouble. If someone especially wanted to act a character it was done over again. Playing at flying birds, jumping animals, and creeping insects, the children represented the things God created.

The sand-table was often prepared to act out a story for the older boys and girls to see, also the parents. When portraying an Easter story they decided the boys and girls should be placed there too. Their attendance chart had stickers of boys and girls "coming to Jesus." They filled the Easter garden with figures of children, making it more beautiful for the teacher, especially when they added clay birds and animals. The children were sure they had all come to see Jesus on that glad morning.

The animals in the Christmas stable were given turns being close to the Baby Jesus. The children made paper models to set up at home for home worship.

To interest them in praying for children of other lands and races, they were shown the picture of our Lord surrounded by children of all colors. Then they were told the story of "The Artist Who Forgot Four Colors." Afterwards a simple poem prayer about all children was used, and copies given for home learning and use.

Drawing and painting is dramatizing a story to a small child. One boy who had heard the story of how the mothers brought their children to Jesus was given a picture of the group to color. He said, "This lady likes blue dresses and this girl wants dresses the color of her hair. The sun likes Jesus and shines on Him most." The figure of Jesus was then colored all yellow, even the face. That boy was acting out the story in color—living it as if he was there, being one of the children near Jesus—worshipping Him in his own simple, adoring way.

How alive and colorful and worshipful our teaching may be with dramatization, but how often we teachers lose our opportunities. We give things adult meanings instead of seeking for the child's needs and meanings. The yellow face of Jesus was glory, not sacrilege, to the small boy. Being a Christian was real and happy, and Jesus was a Friend whom even the sun loved most.

How grateful those children were to their Rector one day. A dog wandered into church and was no respecter of form. The pupils were worried about what the adults would do about the disturbance. They were probably chiefly worried about what would happen to the happy dog. The Rector released cheerful smiles by saying, "Let him stay. God likes dogs, too, and this is God's House." He understood that you can't teach that God created, loves, and receives the worship of all things, and then contradict it, without creating resentment and destroying worship.

One thing we realized over and over again—the smaller the child the greater the capacity for true worship, also the more easily it may be destroyed by blundering adults who forget that God is always present. Our Lord knew these great truths and gave us a stern warning. The responsibility is great but very satisfying when right teaching brings its revelations back to us as it did in the yellow face of Jesus which the small boy colored.

3. PRIMARY GROUP WORSHIP

In discussing how best to help the children of the primary department to feel and enjoy the reality of worship we had several things in mind: (1) Their need to prepare for entering junior and senior worship services with understanding and appreciation. (2) Their need to serve in a widening circle of world fellowship through Christian family motives. (3) Their need to learn to plan and lead some of their own activities in both worship and service. (4) A need to feel important in their own immediate Church family group for both the older and younger boys and girls.

Again we decided to base all on a worship theme and we chose the Apostles Creed for this group. This would be used in all the older worship services and it could either grow to be mere form and words, or a deeply increasing pledge of faith and allegiance to the Christian cause. We found afterwards that some educators were critical of us for using such a deep subject of theology for such young children. However, we decided that what a child was taught to repeat in worship needed to have some meaning for him or her, or we were harming that child's worship. It did not have to be the adult meaning, but it must have a meaning that was real, or it was useless or harmful. How little we realized how much it was needed, and how thankful we were afterwards that we had dared to try to meet this need. The full results of those children's facing of life's problems and of their facing of the next life we will never know, nor the results of their eliminating useless fears. We only glimpsed amazing possibilities.

Taken as a whole, the creed is a statement of belief in our Lord and in His life and teachings. The companionship of our Lord was the need of a primary child as he or she adjusted to developing character and to personal decisions towards life.

As in the kindergarten, we decided to take each clause separately as we had with the Lord's Prayer. We chose simple pictures for almost every clause, leaving a few to their imaginations. The suggestion of each having his own booklet to take home when finished, also one for someone else, again seemed to please them. The covers were also left to individual taste and meaning, except that the words "My Faith" were printed on each as a reminder that it was a personal and not just a congregational faith imposed on them.

Because any faith or loyalty must begin with the person to whom it is given, we decided to probe for the ideas about our Lord which home and any past teaching had given to them. Some of the mothers had spoken of questionings and confusion and fears, and the third-graders had shown much irreverence. This irreverence was a combination of the age of "showing off," which all children go through, and of a lack of interest in worship which had been general according to observed actions.

When questioned, one small girl stated as her definition of prayer, "That is when you talk to God but He is so far off He can't hear you." Too many hymns had statements like "above the bright blue sky," for small minds to understand the theology of heaven being all around us, as our Lord taught it. Some hymns were evidently separating children from God quite seriously.

We decided to take one of the offending hymns they loved for other reasons, and talk about it. We chose "I think when I read that sweet story of old." They knew the words from many singings, so we talked about the author, Jemima Luke. Her first name seemed amusing, so we talked about how ideas changed with each set of fathers and mothers. This led naturally to the suggestion that people learned more and more about what our Lord really meant. We told how Jemima Luke's idea of where the kingdom of heaven was would have been different if she had lived now, how she wrote the hymn about her own longings, how she wanted to see Jesus. In discussing who gave her her name, the Baptismal service was mentioned, and we planned to attend a Baptism later on. A picture of "Jesus and the Children" by Copping, which was hung over the altar, caught the eye of one boy. His brother had recently been baptized. He spoke of the minister taking the children to be baptized in his arms just as Jesus did the children He knew.

This led to the question, "Would you rather have been grown-up or small if you had lived when children could see our Lord and follow Him around?" All but one would have preferred to be grown-up. When asked why, they said that then they could have followed our Lord without having their parents say they couldn't. The one who wanted to be small said she wanted to sit on Jesus' knee as the children did, or to be held by Him like the child in the picture. She had lost her father in death the year before and missed him very much. If we could only make "The communion of saints," "The Resurrection of the body: And the Life everlasting" real to that child's need.

The third verse about prayer brought out questions about where our Lord was now, how we could talk to Him. In talking about what we could talk to Him about, the need of the Church for their prayers, and of theirs for the Church came out. We discussed making our room look beautiful for Him because it was part of His House and we were His family.

Once we got on the subject of heaven, we discovered that it had an absorbing interest for all. Where do people go when they die? If they are alive why can't we see them? The explanation of a body-house with eye windows in this world and of a better new body-house with better windows in the new life, made more satisfying the heaven all about them that the new windows could see. It took the dread out of death for them. It was a real fact to all, even though, as adults, we try to pretend that the idea has not reached the children yet. Children are morbid talkers when they are together. Many had experienced losses that had caused resentment when they were told that God had taken those they loved. It was affecting their prayer life with fears and resentments at an early age. The idea of the new body with the ability to see and know even more, put adventure into death and took out much of the fear. In fact, one teacher said they seemed so eager for their new windows that she hoped they wouldn't commit suicide to get them!

The discussion of the clause referring to the Holy Ghost brought out much misunderstanding about Hallowe'en ghosts being confused with the Holy Ghost. Some children had been threatened with ghosts by ignorant baby-sitters. They feared the Holy Ghost because of this.

One child thought that our Lord literally "sat" on "the right hand of God" and asked if it didn't hurt Him. There were also questions about "the quick and the dead." This seemed to have various meanings from a race, to jumping out of the way of judgment. It showed us that the children were forming their own judgments of what they had heard in Church services.

When one child asked why it was called the Apostles Creed, he was told that the teaching was the one which our Lord had taught His apostles. When they were growing old they wanted to keep all the things He had said safe for us, and so they wrote the stories down. We looked in the Bible and the Prayer Book to find these stories and spoke of the names of the writers.

The children were told how some of the Christians' enemies tried to say wrong things about the Christians to stop them. So, the apostles decided to have a pledge to the cross, just as we have our pledge to our flag to tell about our willingness to serve it and be loyal to it. In their pledge to the cross they began with three things—I believe in God the Father—I believe in God the Son—I believe in God the Holy Ghost.

A question came up about the Holy Ghost and was answered frankly by saying that none of us could understand all about the Holy Ghost until we had our new body-houses. But He is the unseen Friend Jesus promised to send after His death. He helps us by putting right thoughts into our minds when we are willing to do right. He gives us comforting thoughts about God's love if we are afraid or sad. He is always near us, helping us.

Another question asked was whether they would know more about the Holy Ghost when they got to heaven. They were told that Jesus had promised they would and they could trust Jesus. One boy asked if he would know the Indian whose head was on the nickel coin when he got to heaven. He was told that probably he would. His answer was, "Won't it be fun knowing all those people? Did he know about Jesus?" This brought up some teaching about paradise where people would know and understand God better and would meet those they had loved here who had died.

The teacher then asked how people came to know about Jesus, and the group decided that it was by having someone tell them. Then she told them that after a while the shorter creed or pledge was made bigger so that it would tell the story of Jesus and His Church to people who learned the words. The group then read it very slowly. One child asked whether the missionaries used the creed to tell the story, and was told that the missionaries did—that perhaps some day some of them might be doing that too. They then talked of ways they could tell the story now, and offerings were suggested as one way.

The hymn, "All things bright and beautiful," was learned and talked about as being like part of the creed which said, "God the Father Almighty, Maker of heaven and earth." Things the children liked were discussed with pleasure, and this was linked up with thankfulness to God as the Creator.

In addition to separate pictures to illustrate the clauses, the group made a large chart of the creed, adding a picture by each clause, each week, to illustrate it. In this way the meaning grew visually, and children often gathered round the chart before and after the sessions.

In telling about the Annunciation, it was spoken of as God's greatest Gift. The children asked questions about the Virgin Mary and a sand-table model was prepared, as a result, to show what the village of Nazareth and Mary's house might have looked like. From this model of a Nazarene home grew the models of homes of other people, and this continued throughout the year. We made one mistake with this model of Nazareth. The teacher brought and prepared it. Some boys pulled it to pieces to play with the animals, although they didn't touch the figures of Mary and the angel. We asked them to remake it and to bring parts for all the other models, and then all were safe.

Dramatizing stories was very popular with this group in their grade-class spaces. Their imagination did not need costuming and they often used their own words with telling effect. Some gave a simple play about the Resurrection called "Spring in the Brown Meadow," using crepe paper costumes made by the mothers. This was given for the afternoon mothers' group. They dramatized stories of Christmas and Easter in posters for the rest of the school to see. They were also asked to take part in some of the Church pageants of the older groups. In Lent one primary class made a model, each week, of a home in another land. The grades took turns and these were shown to the whole school. Maps dramatized journeys in the stories.

Whenever stories were to be simply dramatized after the telling, the pupils were told before the telling. This had an effect on their listening and made the characters more real to them because they might themselves be those characters afterward. They used some of their dramatizations in place of the service talks at their opening services in the parish house.

This group sometimes created prayers of collected petitions by volunteering things for which to pray. They learned about meditation by sitting with eyes closed and imagining they were "going with our Lord to watch Him teach and heal." They particularly liked doing this in connection with the story of Jairus' daughter when the teacher told the story in their own language. The pictures of boys and girls of other lands, on their Lenten offering boxes, gave them a guide for prayers at home and in school.

They learned to care for their own altar. Two pupils removed the screen from before it, before the service, and replaced it afterwards, as many activities took place in this large room. Two other pupils took up the offering and all said the verse:

> Jesus, bless the gifts we bring Thee,
> Give them something good to do.
> May they help someone to love Thee.
> Jesus, may we love Thee, too.

The third grade planned the positions and hung several religious pictures around the room, choosing two they thought most beautiful (at their own suggestion) for each side of the altar and putting the next most beautiful one in the second-grade room. They kept the one of George Washington for their own room because "He was a good Church man and said his prayers."

Prayers were said by name for ill and absent members, also for the Bishop who had had an accident. The children offered to pray for the Bishop each day at home also.

One grade made a picture for the window for another

grade which was moving into their department "to help them to feel at home." It was a picture of the Good Shepherd. They also planned a party to welcome them and to get acquainted. It was a good opportunity for the teachers, too, and served them.

A Baptismal service in the church, to which the children were invited, was made more meaningful by a previous story of our Lord being baptized. They seemed much impressed by pictures of it. This service was their first regular introduction to the Church Prayer Book. Boys distributed and collected the prayer books and showed everyone where to find the service. One child asked what a hymnal was and learned that it was "the Church's song book." They made crosses to wear home as badges of their discipleship and Church membership. They shared in the Birthday Offering and in the information about its use. They were thrilled by the little model church, so much so, that they sometimes brought extra offerings. Parents helped with models and exhibits also. These models proved very interesting to everyone. They included homes or model villages of the Filipinos, Alaskans, American Indians, Southern Negroes, Chinese, and Japanese. An igloo was made from two halves of a rubber ball covered with cotton. For the Indian village they made pottery bowls of modeling clay and even a clay rattlesnake as "one of the things Indians had to be brave about." The worship for the closing service always included prayers for each group, and the older grade began to read these as leaders. They began to choose their own hymns, too, and to talk about the reasons for and the meaning of the words.

The story of the Church's work with the Southern **Negro** was told very simply and carefully because of the colored sexton and of an appreciation of his very faithful work for the parish for many years. He was part of the parish church to them, and they suggested ways of helping him by putting things away more carefully each week. He was asked to judge the model because he had lived in the South. As a result he asked the director a question he had wanted to ask for years—"Who would be nearest to our Lord in heaven— the colored or the white people?" He was told that whoever followed our Lord's teaching most lovingly and truly. Then he was told the story of "The Artist Who Forgot Four Colors" and the result brought tears to both his eyes and ours. My tears were because he had felt he had had to wait to ask and had never been told as a child. His were tears of relief and happiness.

For the Negro settlement the children made a clay cat, a dog, and a cow. Then they decided the Easter basket grass would be "better for them to eat than sand." They were learning to be kind to God's animals. The dog was placed beside the wood-choppers because "he would like to see the chips fly and to chase them."

When the Easter pageant included Negroes, a colored girl was asked to "have the honor of representing her own race." The girl chosen for the yellow race asked, "Will Jesus be there?" These children also had a part in the Palm Sunday procession, after hearing the story. One of the teachers who had a Chinese costume delighted the children by dressing up in it to review the reasons for the Lenten offering and to remind the pupils to help by bringing their boxes at Easter.

Where visual aids were suitable, this group was included with the whole school. Otherwise, suitable subjects were chosen and shown. This made the people of other lands real for the children's worship and giving.

Because this primary group had not had the teaching about the Lord's Prayer which the kindergarten were receiving, they took that subject as their next unit of work and worship. The same pictures were used, but the questions were different and led us into different teaching of the same truths. The teaching was richer because they had already explored different ways and places in God's kingdom and wanted it "to come." They knew more about what "not forgiving" meant too. Their life situations were more full. The problems of building their own characters needed the guidance of our Lord's prayer. They knew more about "heaven" and why God was called "our" Father. Through their increasing reverence in worship and their caring for the tools of worship they began to sense what "hallowed" meant. They knew that unhappiness came for other people and for themselves when God's will was not "done." They knew that many people were without both spiritual and physical food and that "daily bread" meant both. Temptation was real. We were glad they had the creed and the Lord's Prayer to meet it. They needed both before they were juniors.

IX. TRAINING THE TEACHERS AND LEADERS

1. STAFF TRAINING MEETINGS

This school was an average Church School without paid and without professionally Church-trained teachers except for the Rector and the Director of Religious Education. A director will not be available except to a small proportion of Church Schools who may want to try this plan. That is why this book has been written—so that any school may use it as a director and guide for their own plans. A trained director could undoubtedly manage without these helps, although a sharing of ideas is always spiritually helpful in the Church.

Some of our teachers were office workers, some were housewives and parents, some were businessmen. Some of the assistants were high school girls, but these we preferred to continue in training, and we created a high school teacher and officer training class for them. A few were public school teachers. These had training to give, but needed the special reminders to keep free from the necessarily different discipline so as to allow a more creative approach than their large public school groups made possible, no matter how creatively minded they might be. Sometimes their teacher training was a help and sometimes a hindrance. All of us needed new insights and all of us grew in grace through the year with the boys and girls. The children and young people and our Lord were the teachers. We were guides and counsellors and sometimes almost missed the wise counselling the pupils unconsciously revealed to us. It was a gamble. From the Rector on down we were conscious of two things mainly: (1) The pupils' need of a joy and reality in their worship. (2) That teachers and leaders should be creative evangelists.

We had one general asset. We all saw the problem.

The director did what any Rector or superintendent could do, as a beginning. She gathered the teachers separately by departments to ask their opinions and difficulties, and she noted them down to be dealt with individually if necessary. However, what we all began quickly to see was that the general lack of interest of the pupils was causing all the problems. Each group was asked if they would meet together on the same night once a month for a two-hour staff meeting. If they couldn't come to any one meeting, would they be responsible for finding out what had happened and how it concerned their classes? This didn't always work, so some teachers helped to type a summary and to mimeograph and mail it to all the staff members. Instead of keeping teachers away from the meetings, this summary increased the attendance. They saw that the meetings were becoming interesting and vital. The summaries also helped those who did attend to review things they might have forgotten. Not all teachers are good note-takers, especially while discussion is going on. Also, taking notes limited the freedom of thought for discussion. The summaries were also used as one of the topics for discussion, with the student council's monthly report, for the parents' meeting each month. Teachers were not required to attend the parents' meetings, but most of them did. Sometimes, if the same things were helpful, the staff had a supper meeting before the parents' meeting and joined forces to save time and effort.

Realizing that business can kill the best intentioned of teachers' meetings, we made the following plan: (1) The business should be limited to fifteen minutes. (2) An executive body representing the Rector, director, secretary, treasurer, and one elected teacher from each department, should be appointed to carry on the business of the school and to plan for special conferences. (3) Thirty minutes should be devoted to departmental meetings to discuss vital problems rather than business. (4) The remaining time should be spent as a training class and the particular topic this year should be worship. We all felt that this was the weak place in the school program.

2. A TRUE AND FALSE TEST FOR TEACHERS

To prepare for meeting of the teachers' needs, a true and false test was given at the first training class and used as the basis of future discussions. The main outline was: (1) The teacher's personal experience of worship. (2) The Church School service of worship. (3) Planning future experiences of worship for the Church School. (This was rather taken out of our hands as the pupils realized their abilities to create these plans, but we did have to plan opportunities for their fullest experiences.)

The True and False Test

1. I enjoy the Church School service as a personal experience of worship. (true) (false)

2. I believe in God's presence at the worship service. (true) (false)
3. Hymns help me to understand religion (true) (false)
4. The Rector should always plan the service of worship. (true) (false)
5. The pupils like to pray. (true) (false)
6. The pupils understand the meaning of the hymns. (true) (false)
7. The worship service is connected with most of the lessons prepared by the teacher. (true) (false)
8. The worship service should be shorter. (true) (false)
9. It is important for a teacher to be punctual at a worship service of the Church School. (true) (false)
10. I should watch the members of my class during a worship service. (true) (false)
11. If I see a pupil misbehaving during a service of worship I should speak to him immediately. (true) (false)
12. The worship service is necessary to the spiritual life of my pupils. (true) (false)

These true and false test answers were to be handed in unsigned so that we would be more sure of their honesty. The results were enlightening. Few enjoyed the school service as a personal experience because of the need for discipline. Most teachers thought that the Rector should do all the planning of worship as his right and because it was traditional—not because of the worship. Few thought the pupils liked to pray. All were helped by hymns. None thought the pupils understood the meaning of the hymns. Only one thought the worship was connected with the lesson material and that one was teaching about the Prayer Book. None wanted the service shorter. (I wondered whether because of the worship need or because the lesson period endurance would then be longer.) All thought it important to be punctual. (They became much more so.) None thought they should watch their pupils during a service (that was encouraging), and only one thought they should discipline during the service. All felt the worship service was necessary to spiritual life.

This was a fine base from which to guide the discussions. Before the school began its student council, personal conferences were held with each teacher. Most of them were timid about class supervision or observation, but were willing to have the director take over occasionally to explain special projects and request class help. They were also willing to have occasional training-class reporters. These were the high school pupils in training. They reported to their class, and to the director, chiefly the actions and reactions of the pupils to the teaching. This helped all of us.

3. OTHER TEACHER ACTIVITIES

The student council report was often used at the teachers' meetings, and one teacher was appointed to attend the council meetings and report back to the group. This was also done for the parents' group so that we might have regular reporting. Some of the teachers, with more time, had class teas for the mothers of their pupils and these helped both. The parish bulletin news, plus the occasional form letters and mimeographed reports of parents' meetings, were counted on to create an interest in indifferent or antagonistic parents. However, all parent problems were also reported to the Rector as his pastoral responsibility.

We were teachers in training and, except for the general seasonal planning, we faced things as they came up. The special personal conferences, interest in the library, and a new alertness in observation for problems to bring to our training time, all helped. An adult class in the Church School which was taught by the Rector interested parishioners in training for teaching. Some parents became interested in teaching as the council creativeness progressed and as it interested them in the need. The mimeographed reports of the groups were sent to the vestry and interested them, especially some who were teachers of boys. News of our worship activities permeated the community, and other parish groups wanted reports and a speaker. Some teachers came from these groups. This gave us a supply of substitutes in training.

Instead of discouraging teachers, the interest grew and the attendance steadied. The opportunity for a Sunday off, when the school had special services once a month, was appreciated even when not used. This plan made it easier to secure the right teachers also. Husbands and wives did not object when they knew that, once a month, they could make family plans to drive out of town. The reports coming back were that the pupils actually objected at being taken away from their interest in the services.

The parents car corps also helped to take teachers and officers to district and diocesan leaders' conferences, and several teachers wanted to attend summer schools by the end of the school year.

A primary and kindergarten group started to meet at eleven o'clock for those children who had to come with their parents when they went to Church. This meant a further need for teachers. It also meant including them in the same creative program, although this group missed many of the earlier morning opportunities and had to have their own interest stimulated in occasional part-time visits to the adult congregation when special services were held suitable for children.

One of the main results of value was a new spirit of fellowship and helpfulness between the members of the staff. They knew that the whole parish was behind them and knew about their work. They were building the future Church and they were important. The teachers felt their own lack of Church knowledge and began to read for the special activities of their classes. They began to be more creative and selective in their teaching.

The pupils challenged all of us to do our best. They also humbled us and sent us to the Source of strength and courage. The new interest in the pupils made us realize once again the truth of Christ's edict, "And I, if I be lifted up, will draw all men unto me."